EMPTY NEST TO LIFE VEST

Empty Nest to Life Vest

Plotting a New Course

Christie Gordline

INKWATER PRESS

PORTLAND • OREGON
INKWATERPRESS.COM

Copyright © 2010 by Christie Gorsline
www.christiegorsline.com

Cover and interior design by Masha Shubin

Cover image © Alexander Lechler. DreamsTime.com

All rights reserved. No part of this book may be reproduced or transmitted in any form or by any means whatsoever, including photocopying, recording or by any information storage and retrieval system, without written permission from the publisher and/or author. Contact Inkwater Press at 6750 SW Franklin Street, Suite A, Portland, OR 97223-2542. 503.968.6777

www.inkwaterpress.com

ISBN-13 978-1-59299-504-2
ISBN-10 1-59299-507-7

Publisher: Inkwater Press

Printed in the U.S.A.
All paper is acid free and meets all ANSI standards for archival quality paper.

1 3 5 7 9 10 8 6 4 2

Dedicated to Marv and Chieko on s/v *Endurance* for their cruising spirit and circumnavigation

This book is –

    An authentic and intriguing exploration,
    a perspective on living your intended purpose
    and a **promise**. Life happens once. Enjoy it.

Live your best life....

Christie Gorsline

Muchas, muchas gracias –

to the Judges of the Willamette Writers Kay Snow 2009 nonfiction contest for demonstrating their belief in my writing through a First Place award for *Dolphin Messengers*

to my McCall, Idaho, writing pals who first critiqued the earliest drafts – Bobbie, Berni, Linda, Craig, Dixie and Dawn. And kudos to my Portland writer friends – Joyce, Mary and Carol for encouragement and advice

to Oregon Colony House for their rustic writer hideaway where I went to get back on task

to my editors – Karen Brees and Joanna Rose

to photo guru – Lee Zinsli

to AmyJean and Lisa for growing up so nicely without me nearby. I applaud you both. It's a joy to watch you following your own dreams

to my parents for raising me with confidence

and to Rick for introducing me to a life with so much to say.

> Viajamos con vida en los manos
> del Dio – We travel through
> life in the hands of God.

Contents

Ch. 1.	Silence	1
Ch. 2.	Dropping Out	6
Ch. 3.	Learning	14
Ch. 4.	Departure	26
Ch. 5.	Landfall	45
Ch. 6.	Scribbles	57
Ch. 7.	Cruising	63
Ch. 8.	Life at Sea	72
Ch. 9.	Baggage	89
Ch. 10.	Alive	97
Ch. 11.	*Bahía Banderas*	107
Ch. 12.	South to *Zihuatanejo*	125
Ch. 13.	Exploring	144
Ch. 14.	Spice and Spirit	158
Ch. 15.	Navidad	166
Ch. 16.	Going Home	177
Ch. 17.	Sea of Dreams	194

Ch. 18. Off the Boat 213
Ch. 19. The Storm 228
Ch. 20. Changing Course 235
Epilogue: Patterns from Scraps 243

> *"A journey is like marriage. The certain way to be wrong is to think you control it."*
> — JOHN STEINBECK

CHAPTER 1
Silence

BOULDERS THE SIZE of freighters protected the entrance to the anchorage. A breeze swirled high above the cliffs but our sails hung like limp laundry. I monitored the depth sounder from the nav station, calling out the readings in fathoms, while Rick steered and the diesel engine churned.

And then our world went quiet. Silence. With neither a sputter nor a gasp, *Nanook*'s engine had quit. The quiet throbbed in my ears and clutched at my throat. I took the companionway stairs in a leap.

"Get some canvas up," Rick hollered.

"There isn't any wind," I said, unfurling the jib anyway.

"I know, but it can't hurt." Rick said while he swung the tiller toward me, "Here, take it. Point us out to sea." He disappeared down the companionway. In one smooth motion he lifted the stairs, clipping them to the bracket on the mahogany roof liner to gain access to the engine room. It took less than two minutes but felt like an eternity.

I pushed the tiller hard to port and held it there. Without wind or motor, we were at the mercy of the Pacific Ocean. *Nanook*'s bow inched clockwise toward open water but it looked as if we were also ghosting backward, our stern inching closer to the rocks.

Our engine had overheated since we'd bought *Nanook*. We'd tried everything we could afford in a vain attempt to fix it. This was the first time it had abandoned us. The timing was terrifying.

Clanking noises emerged from the engine room. A loud "Damn it!" was followed by a pause and then a louder "Son of a bitch!"

I winced. The next sound was metal hitting metal. Rick had probably thrown a tool at the devil.

"Is it going to start?" I called. Long minutes of silence ticked by and fear crawled up my spine. My lunch rose in my throat. I glared at the relentless blue sky and the miles of darker blue ocean as if an answer might come from above or below. I feathered the tiller, giving it small back-and-forth strokes, hoping the movement would propel us forward like a swimmer's flutter kick.

I picked up the book Rick had been reading and tore out the title page. Feeling silly, I crumpled it into a ball and tossed it over the stern rail. I couldn't remember what the instructor in my weather class had said about wave patterns close to shore, but I hoped the wad of paper would float out to sea, telling me that the current was pulling us away from shore.

My teeth clenched. Tension radiated down my body. Knots tightened in my shoulders and even my toes were curled firmly, grasping the teak deck. I peered over my left shoulder trying to figure out whether the distance to the rocks was shrinking or growing. The ball of paper bounced next to us, moving up the port side, which gave me hope.

In the two years we'd been at sea, I had often whined about the diesel motor's oily smell and growling noise. Now I pledged to the gods above that I would never again complain about the motor if it would just start this one time.

Rick's voice interrupted my prayers. "Honey, do you know where we put the engine repair manual?"

"Oh my God. You're gonna read?" I asked.

"Not if I can't find the book."

"Top bookshelf, starboard side, aft section." Some things I was sure of. The sight of Rick calmed me for the few moments I could see his brown eyes and tanned shoulder through the hatch opening. When he turned away, my panic returned, like loud music after a short intermission.

"Okay, I found it. Give me a few minutes."

I talk when I'm scared and to be honest, even when I'm not. We'd been married for sixteen years, so Rick should have known it was a ridiculous request. I needed something to do if I was going to give him time alone with the blasted Volvo repair manual.

I lashed the tiller in place and went forward. Raising the main sail, I sheeted it in. Back in the cockpit, I feathered the tiller again. The balled-up book page bobbed amidships like a little tug boat.

My head swiveled. I squinted at the sail, wishing for wind to fill it, and then over my shoulder at the rocks on the Mexican coast. Back and forth, like watching a tennis match, my eyes willing us out to sea.

When we'd dreamed up this sailing adventure, we'd thought of it as a time-out to travel and to re-prioritize our lives. A circumnavigation hadn't seemed like an impossible plan and we'd spent two years preparing ourselves and *Nanook*. We'd taken sailing classes, replaced the sails and electronics, repaired the aging motor and studied celestial navigation.

But now it didn't feel like enough.

A sputter from the engine shattered my reverie.

"Almost got it," Rick called. A few more false starts and the engine roared to life. Rick put the stairs back down and came up into the cockpit, his hands dark with spattered oil. "Bled the fuel lines again," he said, leaning down to give me a peck on the nose.

The tears that had threatened to spill now fell in relief. Streams ran down my cheeks and chin. Rick wiped the waterworks from my jaw and gave me an awkward hug, holding his dirty hands away. I sighed, leaning into his chest, and relaxed my grip on the tiller.

"I'm sorry I'm such a ninny," I hiccupped.

"Nothin' to be sorry about. That was definitely no fun."

"Do you want me to turn around and we'll try the anchorage again?"

"Nahh." Rick said. "I'll scrub my hands and get the chart. Keep us on this course and I'll check out options south of here."

A few minutes later, with clean hands, Rick came up the companionway with two plastic glasses filled with red box wine and the chart book clamped under his elbow.

"You're just what the doctor ordered," I said, reaching for the glass with my free hand. "Where should we go?"

We examined the chart book and decided on a marina about forty miles south. We figured we'd be there by lunch the next day.

> "Take the adventure, heed the call, now, ere the irrevocable moment passes...Then someday, someday long hence, jog home here if you will, when the cup has been drained and the play has been played and sit down by your quiet river with a store of goodly memories for company."
>
> KENNETH GRAHAME,
> THE WIND IN THE WILLOWS

CHAPTER 2

Dropping Out

WHEN RICK MARRIED me, he got three of us. Lisa was five and AmyJean eight. Over the next decade he was a wonderful father to the girls and the right partner for me, but mismatched for his career. He worked in management at car dealerships and the long hours and lack of integrity by upper management had left him disillusioned.

With the girls in their teens and choosing colleges, Rick saw their budding independence as an opportunity for us. He wanted a break from the angst of deal making. He needed time off that was longer than two weeks.

I agreed that we should take a sabbatical of sorts, a chapter break between parenting and whatever came next. My work life had never settled into what could be called a career. It was more like a stream of jobs. I'd sold coupon advertising, worked in an advertising agency, in a doctor's office, for a stockbroker, as a travel agent, and

I'd taught high school English and Journalism. But my favorite moniker was "Mom."

During one of our frequent discussions about what form the change should take, I said, "Sweetheart, you've given all these years to being a Dad and making us a family. The next decade should be yours." I don't know if I meant it, but I did say it.

En route to our decision to go sailing, we explored countless versions of a plausible time-out. We talked about renting a house in Europe or buying an RV and touring the United States. We entertained the notion of buying an open-jaw, around-the-world plane ticket. Discarding the ideas that were either too expensive, too mundane, or more of a trip than a lifestyle change, we decided on a sailing circumnavigation.

The first hurdle was that we didn't own a boat and never had.

We'd chartered boats, both power and sail, for family vacations, but we weren't sailors. My curiosity about life on the ocean sent me to the library to read every sailing adventure story on the shelves. Tales of trade winds, white sand beaches and waving palm trees made me optimistic, but books that appeal to publishers are about storms, months in a life raft and imminent disaster. I pummeled Rick with questions, wanting him to assure me that nothing bad would happen.

Would we learn to navigate by the stars? Would we sink if we hit a whale? How would we stay in touch with our daughters and parents? How would we get mail?

What if one of us got hurt? Or sick? To most of my questions, Rick shrugged and smiled, indicating that he didn't have a clue.

While he couldn't promise that all our days would have Walt Disney endings, the idea of making a significant change intrigued me. With the girls headed to college I was getting the proverbial pink slip from the job I had liked best. My hope was that an adventure would work like a chisel, carving a new identity and purpose while I was still young enough to pursue new dreams. Even to my idealistic self, it felt like a high benchmark.

Part of the appeal of going sailing was that we'd belong to a community of fellow cruisers, anchoring next to like-minded couples and chatting on the radio. That appealed to my sense of neighborhood.

I pictured us lolling along the world's waterways in a floating version of home, sort of like a motor home on water. A decade later, I found the flaw in the analogy. RVers drive on highways with signs pointing to where they should park. Boats have to search the openings between rocks for an entrance to a harbor, reading ocean charts to get that far. RVs don't drag the anchor when the wind picks up. Four wheels are simply more stable than a canoe-shaped hull. Fortunately, none of that occurred to me while we were in the planning stages.

I pictured my little sailboat with a symbolic likeness to the fort where my friend Sue and I hung out in the summer after fifth grade. We lay on our backs with our legs sprawled out on the plywood floor. The sunlight filtered through the trees and onto our youthful, hairy legs. We talked with great seriousness about when we would start shaving. We shared secrets about what we would do when we were all grown up, maybe at twenty. Now I was close to fifty and planning to live in a floating version of that fort. With shaky logic grounded in lack of experience, it all made sense.

At our first "Basics of Boating" class the instructor asked the students to introduce themselves, their boats and their experience. When it was our turn, we eagerly announced, "We don't have a boat yet, but we're going to buy one and sail around the world." Laughter erupted from the room of knowledgeable boaters. We were confident, but apparently naïve.

We joined a local sailing club and began weekend chartering. Since we lived two hours from the ocean and the girls were in high school, this was a major commitment. We went to boat shows, walked miles of docks and asked questions. We read magazines and talked to boat brokers.

When we first saw *Nanook* we agreed that she was elegant below decks and sturdy enough to go where we planned. Rick liked her low freeboard and price. I was entranced by the warm wood in the cabin that shone like maple syrup. She had a tiller instead of a wheel and green canvas instead of marine blue. Her name appealed to us, too. *Nanook* is the Inuit Indian word for polar bear and with her off-white hull and canoe stern, from behind she did look like a polar bear's butt. She was a fifteen-year-old thirty-seven–foot Crealock, Pacific Seacraft, cutter design. All of this appealed to us and soon she was ours.

I broke a bottle of champagne over the bow. Rick snapped a picture and we started another kind of list. The engine needed tuning. We would replace the sails, buy a dinghy, upgrade the out-of-date electronics and learn to sail.

Our daughters, parents, friends and co-workers all had a different perspective about our plan to abandon suburbia. Some thought we were lucky to be going on an adventure, but the majority of my co-workers told me I was crazy to give up the security of a house, job and accumulated treasures.

I responded to their misgivings by saying that going sailing meant seeing who I might become besides the

"Mom" I'd always been. I saw a neighbor at the mailbox and told her what we were planning. I think I used the words, "We're going to sail around the world in search of new ways to live." The look on her face was as puzzled as if I'd announced that we were going to Tibet to become monks.

We told our daughters we were searching for what to do with ourselves since they had moved on. They took it in stride. I told my parents we wanted to have an adventure, which was fine with them as long as we came back and Rick went back to work within a year or two. A friend of Rick's described our choice to abandon suburbia in more specific terms. We were going to "sell the farm and eat the chickens."

Once the die was cast, my progression from suburban homemaker to expatriate took on a life of its own. I filled boxes with sweaters, formal wear and shoes. An assortment of kitchen tools that hadn't been out of the drawer since we'd last moved joined the pile. Some of the accumulation went to the local thrift store and the rest I put in the garage to be sold at a yard sale. I spent an entire summer deciding and making piles. Nothing in the house was immune to rejection.

We sold Lisa's bunk bed and desk while she was working at a camp the summer before she left for college. I examined every knickknack for future importance. With the logic that my next house, whenever I had one, would probably be smaller and that I would most likely amass new trinkets during our travels, I ruthlessly added to the boxes marked "sell." It was a satisfying liberation that became addictive. I filled trash bags and more boxes. Each shedding amplified the intensity of the change we were plotting.

The clutter of belongings on card tables in the garage was clear evidence of forty-five years of living. I stuck bits of masking tape on the assemblage. Rick's old golf bag might bring $2, the kids' boogie boards $1 each and everything on the small card table I had marked 50 cents "or best offer." A pretty red-checked platter I'd used for the last dozen years was chipped. I wrote $3 on it. Selling everything that was once important was a bit like walking on ice. I was sliding into uncharted territory.

Our relationship to things changes as we grow older. When I was young, I didn't care what bauble was on the coffee table. I waited impatiently while my parents fussed over buying a lavender hurricane lamp or another piece of brass or copper for their growing collection. My brother and I pulled at their sleeves, wanting to play in the sand or go to the ice cream store while they debated exactly where the treasure would be enthroned when we got home.

As I grew older, I entered an acquisition phase to fill my own house. The growing accumulation represented independence and emerging adulthood. When I had children, my belongings expanded to include cribs and strollers and later to prom dresses and letterman jackets.

But going sailing meant emptying the nest. Regardless

of the nostalgia for a collection of old 78s or a once-prized trophy, I needed to move on. If I was going to remodel my life, the first step was to clear the building site.

My series of yard sales consumed five Saturdays. One by one, my belongings marched down the driveway and out of my life. A customer wanted both bicycles for $20. I nodded and pocketed the bill. My piano left on a trolley and tears slid down my cheeks. I had a pocketful of cash and a nearly empty house.

It reminded me of the day when furniture, photos and boxes of belongings had walked out the door and into a moving van with my first husband. He took a small truckload and left me with extra closet space, empty hangers, dents in the carpet and two toddlers. With my ex-husband's share of the furniture gone, the girls rode their tricycles in the living room. Then, as now, it was things, or the shedding of them, that lay the groundwork for a major change. The spaces echoed and I wondered if it was the accumulation of goods that had held me captive.

> *"I know of no more encouraging fact than the ability of a man to elevate his life by conscious endeavor."*
>
> HENRY DAVID THOREAU

CHAPTER 3

Learning

LIVING ON *NANOOK* in the Long Beach, California, harbor, we spent weekends doing boat repairs. Monday through Friday we had land jobs. Each deposited paycheck inched us closer to what we thought of as D-day, Departure Day. We drew lines through boxes on the calendar to note the passage of time but the boat projects multiplied like bacteria, threatening to move the start of our new lives into Never Never Land.

Five mornings a week Rick rode his motorcycle south along the Pacific Coast Highway for a pre-dawn racquetball game en route to work. After a solo cup of coffee, I scurried down the gangway, heading for the shower building housed in the parking lot.

The marina was silent except for the whoosh of wings as a brown pelican lifted off from one piling and landed on another. Silhouettes of slim gray ghosts, their tall masts pointing skyward in the gloom, waited for warm afternoons and light breezes. Only then would happy chatter transform the marina into a carnival. On a winter weekday morning it was quieter than a deserted church.

I stopped at my car to collect a terrycloth bath towel and work clothes. For a live-aboard boater, the car is a closet. Towels dried fast draped over the passenger seat and clothes hung unwrinkled from a rod across the back.

There was nothing fancy about the marina's bathroom. I mused that prison inmates probably had more luxurious digs, but my concrete stall was mine by choice. I dressed and drove into south Los Angeles where I taught high school English and Journalism.

The teenagers in my classes led lives that were totally foreign to anything I had experienced. None had two-parent homes. Most of the boys had parole officers and the girls who didn't have babies wanted them. I didn't know how to relate. When I was a teenager I played golf. My students knew the rules of street survival. I wondered if they were teaching me more than I could teach them.

A few of my students visited me at the marina, intrigued by their teacher who lived on a sailboat. We walked along the water's edge and talked in a way I couldn't duplicate at school. I wanted to give them the spirit of possibility. I know I tried.

Evenings and weekends we chipped away at upgrading *Nanook*. I crawled around on my hands and knees varnishing, caulking seals and tightening bolts.

Rick attached mast steps, a windvane steering system and a steaming light. We worked together to attach a blipper to the mast. It would send a signal to the radar of a passing boat making us a bigger "blip" than we really were. My split fingernails and chapped hands were proof of my efforts. Most Sunday evenings we crossed off a half dozen projects but the list invariably grew with just as many new tasks.

Returning from a Saturday trip to the local marine supply store, Rick said, "When I opened my wallet, there was a loud sucking sound."

I laughed. The outpouring of money reminded me of the old sailor quip that b-o-a-t stands for "break out another thousand," and it was true. Sometimes we lost sight of the dream and could only see tired sails, aged electronics, leaking portholes, a quirky engine and classes to take. Despite the internal storms that sometimes threatened to submerge us, we marched forward, completing projects as efficiently as we knew how.

Lisa and AJ came home for the summer and *Nanook* got even smaller. They slept on the settees in the main salon and stored their gear in the cockpit and cars. They both took college classes at a nearby community college. AJ worked for a neighborhood newspaper and Lisa got a job at the Sheraton across the street from the marina. We were a family again except for the three weeks I went to Mexico for a Spanish immersion school.

Our time frame for departure was a moving target. Rick wanted to wait another year or two so we could

build up our cruising kitty. Delaying was fine with my conservative self but not with the adventuresome woman I itched to unleash. I could hear her knocking on my skull for her chance to act out. She wanted to cut loose and take life as it came instead of spending more time planning and getting ready.

Rick was justifiably worried about our diesel engine. If we kept working, we could replace it. I argued that there would always be a reason to go "next year." I was on a teeter-totter, rocking between go and wait, afraid that there would always be another repair project we should tackle and that in the end we wouldn't go at all.

Rick was the idea man in our twosome and once we agreed on something, which was lots of the time, I became the go-getter who pushed the plan to completion. That had been our chemistry for home remodeling and family vacation ideas as long as we'd been together. I reasoned that going cruising was just a much more massive beast than what color to paint the dining room or the choice between Lake Powell and Lake Shasta for a vacation.

Nanook was thirty-seven feet long and eleven feet wide, but she got smaller when we argued. On our good days we were co-conspirators, working toward a common goal, but when we disagreed, we didn't sound or feel like lovers headed off on an adventure. I whined and Rick silenced me with a look that could strip varnish. Live-aboard angst combined with our separate reasons for overloaded nerves and frustration. When it was least appropriate, I channeled the mess into words and flung the package like daggers at the nearest target. Rick. Our fights were loaded with more than a decade of goodies, our plates piled higher than a Las Vegas buffet.

Within the confines of *Nanook* we played out the discord of Venus and Mars, timid versus adventurer, sparring partners who doubled as lovers. One Friday evening, over beers at our favorite tavern, toasting the end of the work week and the beginning of another boat project weekend, we established a middle ground.

Prepping an old boat to go cruising was like painting the Golden Gate Bridge, a never-ending project. We would go when we were almost ready because the day we would be completely ready would never come. We clicked our frosty beer mugs, toasting the truce.

By Christmas, AJ had finished her semester abroad and left London to explore Eastern Europe. Lisa was with us on the boat and we wrapped the mast with a string of lights, trying to pretend we were in the suburbs for a sense of normalcy. On Christmas morning AJ called from Poland.

Rick and I approached the United States Power Squadron's list of classes with the dedication of high school students attacking a college prep curriculum. Starting with "Basics of Boating," we learned sailing theory and the dynamics of wind movement in the sails. We studied the physical aspects of sailing, marlinespike seamanship (tying knots) and basic navigation rules. We even took "Introduction to Heavy Weather Sailing." I was a good sport but I didn't think it was necessary because I planned to avoid what they described as "heavy weather."

We enrolled in a "Boating Safety" class that emphasized the importance of wearing a life vest harness. These inflatables hung around our necks and were equipped with tethers that snapped with a carabiner to a pad eye on the deck or mast depending on where on the boat we needed to anchor ourselves. We attached strobe lights and whistles for extra insurance.

In a simulated man-overboard exercise, the instructor tossed a coconut overboard and started yelling and pointing at it. I turned, saw it and then it disappeared in the trough of waves. The students turned the boat around, which is more complicated and slower than simply spinning a steering wheel. We searched the sea for Mr. Coconut Head but we never found him.

The demonstration sealed the deal. Falling overboard would mean almost certain death and that didn't figure into our plans. We vowed to wear our life vests and to snap-shackle ourselves to the boat whenever seas were rough or one of us asleep or below deck.

By the end of our first year of preparation we'd learned to plot a course on the chart, to convert magnetic to true north, to plot direction and distance and to use dead reckoning. It was all excellent theory from the inside of a classroom. I could do the plots and pass the exams but the real test would be on the ocean.

We sailed to Catalina Island every time the weather was decent and we had two days off. It was good practice. I plotted the course and could steer a decent track. I'd figured out which way the winch cranked and I handled the sails with growing confidence. I could steer us into the wide anchorage but never back into the slip at the marina. It scared me that I still hadn't been on watch at night and I wasn't surprised that Rick out-performed me in every aspect of what we'd learned in our classes.

We took a one-week vacation, sailing to the unpopulated back side of Catalina Island. We fell immediately asleep on a bright sunny afternoon. I woke up to the sound of the ship's clock clanging. One, two, three. I rubbed my eyes. It couldn't be three in the morning but it was too dark to be 3:00 PM. The pewter twilight was more like dusk on a rainy day. I climbed into the cockpit;

we were enshrouded in a veil of dense fog. Peering over the railing, I wondered how many boats were out there. I couldn't see the bow.

When the fog lifted, I saw that we were alone. It was an odd sensation, like thinking you're in a crowded theatre but when the lights come on you're the only one there.

A CIRCUMNAVIGATION COMES with a long list of entry ports. That meant an equally long list of required immunizations. Los Angeles County offered a low-cost package so we drove to the gray cinderblock building, took a number and picked up two clipboards with pens attached. Sitting in chairs that looked as if they'd been around the world themselves, we began to tackle the forms.

We made our way down our separate questionnaires, conferring to be sure we checked all the same boxes. South America and Africa required shots for the yellow fever mosquito. Symptoms to watch for in tropical zones were described as nausea and pain that subsides after several days except in some patients who contract a toxic phase. Liver damage with jaundice, giving the little critter its name, can lead to death. Death was not in our immediate plans.

There were shots for dengue fever but the literature advised that the painful shot and the swelling it might cause could be avoided if "travelers stay in hotels or resorts that are well screened or air conditioned and that take measures to reduce the mosquito population." That could have read simply, "Stay home." *Nanook* didn't qualify as a resort and certainly wasn't air conditioned. We got the shots.

Most of the vaccines were given in a series over a period of days or weeks. We returned to the clinic with such regularity that it began to feel like a second home. At every visit we were handed more brochures describing the horrors of contracting malaria, rabies and complicated-sounding diseases I'd never heard of and we hoped to avoid. We set a schedule to get more shots in the future because we wouldn't reach some destinations for at least a few years.

I took classes to earn my Ham radio license and we both got scuba certified. Rick studied celestial navigation and learned to read the positions of the sun and stars and a method of sight reduction to plot our position.

Acknowledging that our safety and comfort would be weather dependent, I signed up for a weather class. Once a week for two and a half months I drove across town and sat on a cracked yellow vinyl chair at the instructor's gray Formica kitchen table and learned the basic principles of meteorology. Along with three other students, all men, I listened to how weather systems form, behave, move and interact.

We studied color photographs and drawings of clouds and the nature of sun pillars caused by ice crystal reflection. I learned about relative humidity, dew point and supersaturation. Discussions about the ITCZ, the

Intertropical Convergence Zone, and trade wind patterns warmed my enthusiasm and added to my vocabulary if nothing else.

I wasn't sure why I needed this information or how I would use it but I was better at being a student than varnishing teak, so I kept going. In week seven we learned about tropical and subtropical storms. That sounded relevant and I took twice as many notes.

The fantasy of going on this adventure with the man I was married to kept me on track. There was a two-hour test and I passed.

Some aspects of disengaging from society were uglier than others. With no hospitals or ambulances miles from shore, we would be dependent on ourselves. We enrolled in a class called "Medicine at Sea" to learn survival techniques when help could be days away. A length of rubber tubing pulled tight would stop a deadly loss of blood but I shuddered at the thought that I might have to perform the grisly task on Rick or myself. We learned how to strap a broken leg to an oar and brainstormed other handy items like a wood spoon for a forearm and the leeboards for a back.

We outfitted a soft-sided ice chest to use as a medicine kit, filling it with pain killers, needles and thread, burn pastes and bandages. After class one evening, while I graded English papers in the cockpit, Rick practiced giving injections to a lemon and stitching a slashed orange. The dripping orange smelled heavenly but the reason for the exercise and the image of a deep gash oozing blood made me shiver despite the warm evening.

We worked on our cruising budget and after considerable agonizing decided that the health insurance we could afford wouldn't cover us out of the country so it would be useless. Using the doctors in the countries we visited would be our best option, despite how scary that seemed from the comfort of home. We would forgo health insurance and consider ourselves self-insured.

The day the solar panels were installed we celebrated the milestone that being able to live without shore power signaled. That was a high. But when Rick measured the dinghy transom to mount the wheels we would use to drag it to high ground, then drilled the holes in the wrong places, it was a step backward.

I re-caulked the portholes. Before I started, one leaked, but when I finished, four leaked. Sometimes I laughed at our ineptitude, other times I cried. Rick said, "We're leaving everything we know for the unknown, which is exciting. We're also leaving everything we're good at."

In the midst of our preparations, an acquaintance on our dock did the unthinkable. Without any visible angst, John and Janice left on *Dulcinea* for Mexico, making it look too easy. A big difference was that they were sailors and they'd owned their boat for a number of years. It took me awhile to get back on track after they left.

I bought a copy of *Hoyle's Rules of Games*, thinking that when we played cards, *Hoyle* would be the designated judge and jury. "Too bad there isn't a *Hoyle* in all areas of potential marital discord," I muttered to the bookstore sales gal. She just chuckled, not realizing that I was about to set sail into my future with only my husband for company, comfort and conversation. We would need artibtration in more categories than just card games but there wasn't much I could do to prepare for those situations.

Rick was a talented sales manager with authority and responsibility over a large team. I had proven that I could sell advertising and manage a high school classroom. Rick was a tournament racquetball player and low handicap golfer. I was adept at getting food on the table for a family and keeping the house reasonably clean and neat.

Now we were inching closer to the day that we would leave all of that and replace it with a life that was unfamiliar. We would be learners for a very long time.

> "The water pulls like a magnet and so we go to sea, as our ancestors did before us."
>
> ANONYMOUS

CHAPTER 4

Departure

I TRACED OUR route on a world map using a dark red felt tip pen. Beginning in Southern California, the line marched boldly across the indigo spaces that were the world's oceans.

We would travel south to San Diego and down the Mexican Baja. We wanted to spend a year exploring Mexico's coastline and the Sea of Cortez. The rest was conjecture but "the plan" was to visit the Marquesas, Tahiti and on to New Zealand. We wanted to sail around the north side of Australia, to Sri Lanka and through the Suez Canal. Or to Durban, South Africa. The video screen in my head played images of cobblestone walkways and foreign marketplaces waiting for my arrival. We would skip around the world like a stone over water.

Whether we sailed the southerly route around Africa or north through the Suez Canal and the Mediterranean, we would sail the Atlantic, transit the Panama Canal and go north to cross our starting line on the Pacific side of Mexico. Our lap around the world would take a minimum of a half dozen years and maybe twice that long. It sounded huge. I wondered if the plan was bigger than we were.

My parents were horrified that Rick would quit his job before retirement age. I reminded myself that we were adults making our own choices, although their displeasure niggled at me.

Rick quit his job and I resigned, too. We sold the cars and closed all but one bank account. We kept an investment checking account to write checks for our storage unit, to pay the credit card bill and to retrieve cash from ATM machines.

A neighbor came by with a bottle of champagne. We popped the cork and poured the bubbly. Toasting with plastic wine glasses makes an inconclusive thud, but the amber liquid brought out my celebratory instincts and hid my nerves, even from myself. I wrote in our Ship's Log: "Go. Everything from now on is unproductive nervous energy."

Not wanting to leave on a Friday, which is bad luck to boaters and definitely not on Friday the thirteenth; we left the harbor that afternoon. With a toot of the horn we slipped away from our home marina and began our new lives. I stifled a bilge-full of anxiety and Rick steered *Nanook* into open water. It was Thursday, October 12, 1995.

I raised the mainsail, Rick set the jib and self-steering and we reclined in the cockpit. The smog of Los Angeles slowly receded. We stared at each other in wonder. We were cruising.

It was no longer in our future. The tears weren't for what we were leaving but the fact that we were leaving. Years of planning and thousands of dollars had been spent to make this possible.

We'd been at sea for less than an hour when a thumping noise startled me.

"What's that?" I asked Rick.

"What's what?"

"That thunk, chunk sound," I said.

"No idea," Rick was calm and returned to reading his Frederick Forsyth novel.

Late in the afternoon, we dropped the anchor. It was 70 degrees and Rick put on his scuba gear to look for a reason for the clunking noise. While he inspected the hull, I did wifely chores: wiping counters, plumping pillows and starting dinner. I plopped Jimmy Buffett's *Changes in Latitudes* CD in the player. While ginger-orange pork simmered on the propane stove, I sang along with Jimmy.

When Rick clambered back on board and out of his wetsuit, I poured him a glass of juice and told him that the light in the galley didn't work and that the stove wouldn't ignite with the clicker. He started another list, one we would tackle in a few days when we got to San

Diego. We dismissed our worries about the funny noise because we had no way to figure out what it was.

We fell asleep listening to the creak of the rigging and the music of water against the hull.

Motor sailing south the next morning, the sea was flat and calm. The sun crested the horizon, turning the ocean into a giant's puddle of gold. The autopilot was steering and I was topless. We had spontaneous sex on the bow, distracted only by the awareness that a boat might appear. Rick gave the horizon a cursory glance as often as I did, but our privacy was complete. Minutes later, dozens of dolphins cavorted off our starboard bow. Or were they applauding? When they disappeared we put on our clothes to approach San Diego harbor.

Under power and with slack sails flapping, Rick steered us too close to the notorious kelp beds, catching our keel in the tangled mass growing in the shallow water. We didn't want the long grasses to wrap the prop so we shut it down. Without wind we were as good as anchored and felt like idiots.

The dolphins had been fun to watch but weren't the good omen they are supposed to be. No longer feeling smug but rather foolish instead, I sat straddling the bow rigging and tried to move us forward with an oar. Two rescue boats hovered like crows over roadkill just outside the kelp's danger zone. We were too cheap and possibly too proud to call them for a tow. After a few hours, the tide rose and we floated off the shallow beds.

We motored into San Diego harbor and dropped the

anchor. The local radio Net had announced free hors d'oeuvres at Charlie Brown's restaurant so we rowed the dinghy to the restaurant's dock. Munching on free snacks, we looked out across the bay where *Nanook* was anchored.

Getting our news on the VHF radio instead of reading a newspaper or having television was a tangible transition to being full-time boaters. News that related to land-based events was already losing its relevance. We knew there was increasing tension in Chechnya and that NATO was holding the forty-first session of the North Atlantic Assembly but the significance to us was minimal. Our attention was riveted on sailing away.

In the morning I walked to the marina office to collect our first package of mail. It wasn't there. I called our forwarding service in Seattle and they had written it down for the following week. I cancelled that drop and told her I would call again with a General Delivery address in Mexico and hung up. I exhaled. Loudly. Not being in control of details was going to be part of the learning curve. I reminded myself that I was a cruiser now and mail was supposed to lose its importance. "This is not a crisis, it is NOT a crisis" I repeated to myself while I crossed the street.

But another crisis loomed. I was bleeding rectally. Not only was it uncomfortable and embarrassing but we had plans that didn't include a medical problem. We planned to sail south with a group of cruisers that called themselves the Baja HaHa. The annual flotilla created a party atmosphere for new cruisers making the long trip down the coast of the Mexican Baja. We had looked forward to it as a way to make new friends and to comply with the safety in numbers theory for our first ocean passage.

Instead, we took the dinghy to shore and walked to a pay phone. Rick thumbed through the yellow pages under the heading "Physicians, Colon and Rectal." With a pocket full of quarters, I dialed and asked questions.

I got a doctor's appointment later that day and we took the bus to his office. The news was that I needed a sphincterotomy. He could operate the next day. Apparently, I had bleeding, protruding hemorrhoids. Not pretty, but not fatal either.

We'd cancelled our health insurance but we had a checkbook and $4,000 in cash that was earmarked to buy a life raft. It's a safety feature that anyone venturing far from shore is advised to carry. If the boat goes down, the theory is that you want something that pops open and you can step up into as you abandon your boat.

I threw my arms around Rick's neck and cried against his chest. Part of me was relieved that I'd be completely healthy in a week or two. The rest of me hated the idea of spending our life raft money and delaying our cruising plans.

Rick rented a car for my one-day surgery. It went well

and I convalesced bobbing at anchor. Rick inflated the child's pool we brought for washing clothes. He filled it with hot water in the cockpit to make sitz baths for me. He hung a sheet from the awning for privacy and cooked the meals.

We accepted that the dinghy would be our life raft and resigned ourselves to the fact that we wouldn't be going with the HaHa. When the fleet left, we sailed with them as crew on *My Girl*. The fleet headed south and we waved, yelling with all our might, "See you in Mexico." Rick took the helm and under the direction of the skipper, efficiently sailed to catch the mooring without using the motor. Another first.

While we waited for my post-surgery checkup, we took the trolley to the border and walked into Tijuana. We needed a permit in order for my Ham radio license to get the added prefix it needed for use in Mexican waters. It was November 2, the Day of the Dead, a Mexican holiday.

Turning away from the closed government office building, we walked back to town and joined a meandering mass of families carrying trays of food. We couldn't do our errand but no one could stop us from having fun. I accepted a flyer from a man on a street corner in exchange for a peso. The brochure explained *Dia de los Muertos* in English.

It said that a popular Mexican belief is that on the Day of the Dead it's easier for the souls of the departed to visit the living so families go to cemeteries on that day to communicate with the deceased. They build private altars and display favorite foods as well as photos and memorabilia. They sing and dance at the cemeteries with the gusto of Americans celebrating the living. We joined the throngs and partied with them. The cemetery was cast in twilight shadows by the time we headed back toward the border. Magic and the scent of marigolds mingled in the air.

We spent the days of my recovery like misplaced tourists with one foot in the cruising world and the other shopping in retail suburbia. We sold one of our solar panels at a swap meet. I bought new underwear at Nordstrom. We crossed the border again to complete the Ham radio paperwork. Ten days after my operation, I headed for what I hoped was my final doctor appointment. I took the bus to the office and planned to do the last grocery provisioning on my return.

"I've got good news and bad news," my surgeon said. Before I could process the possibilities, he continued. "The good news is that you're healing beautifully. You and Rick can go sailing wherever you were headed when you landed in my office."

"Perfect," I said, clapping my hands like a child at a birthday party.

"And the bad news can be resolved right away," he continued. "My surgical assistant pricked himself with your blood so we need to get you tested."

I brushed it off. "Tell him he's lucky. My blood is clean. I've been with one sex partner for years and years.

But hey, what about me? Is he healthy? Did he get checked?" I was rambling.

The doctor smiled and patted my hand. "He contaminated himself with your blood outside the operating room, you weren't at risk. But you'll need to go to the hospital today so they can draw a sample."

"I rode the bus to get here and we're going cruising tomorrow," I objected. I'm sure I sounded stubborn but I was eager to get going and I didn't have a car.

The doctor told me to wait a minute and when he returned he led me to a waiting ambulance in front of the building. I had my own limousine and chauffeur, under the guise of an ambulance and driver.

After the perfunctory hospital lab blood test I hurried out to my waiting ambulance and clambered into the passenger seat. "Where am I taking you?" the driver asked.

I told him I lived on a cruising sailboat anchored in the harbor but I needed to do a small amount of last-minute provisioning before we left for Mexico. I must have been feeling spunky because I asked him to stop at the grocery store. In the market's parking lot, I tore my list in half and said, "It'll take half as long if you grab these things and I'll get the rest."

Splitting the grocery list and speed shopping through the store was the way my family had shopped on vacation. I remember my little sister getting the easy things on the list and the rest of us with four or five items each racing through the small market at the beach. It had been fun.

In less than twenty minutes, we met at the cash register with our two grocery carts. Loading the bags into the ambulance, I wondered what Rick would think when I waved at him from shore in the company of a white-clad ambulance driver unloading our supplies.

AT 3:00 IN the morning on November 8, we motored out of San Diego harbor, passing Coronado Island, the USS *Kitty Hawk* aircraft carrier and the Navy Seals training corps. We sailed into open ocean with fifteen knots of wind off the port bow. My original jitters were gone and I felt confident that what we didn't know we would figure out. We would certainly have the time.

Rick was trimming the sails in a light breeze when the water on both sides of the boat bubbled and boiled. A dozen dolphins vaulted in and out of the sea in arcs like rainbows. I ran to the bow and leaned over the rail to get a closer look. In twos and threes they leapt out of the ocean to stand on their tails and pirouette. I threw back my head and laughed with pure joy. The synchronized swimmers entertained us for nearly an hour and then vanished with a flash of fins and a flip of their tails. Like the curtain rising on a musical, our lives at sea had begun.

We sat together on the bow and watched the red ball of the sun sink into the ocean. The winds were light,

so our speed hovered around four knots. I tried to help adjust the sails but couldn't remember which way the winch cranked. "Clockwise, clockwise, remember what you learned in class," I reminded myself.

I set the cockpit table with plastic plates and glasses for practicality, but also with woven place mats and bright cloth napkins. After all, this was our home. The aroma of pasta with canned mushrooms and sun-dried tomatoes, garlic bread and red wine blended with the sea air while the stars clicked on in the darkening sky.

When Rick went below to get some sleep, I took my first turn on night watch. I snapped my harness to the cockpit sole using the tether with its carabiner attached. A knot tightened in my chest and I berated myself for what I still didn't know. There was a lot of wiggly water out there and I was in charge.

Rick poked his head through the companionway and reminded me that if the wind strengthened and I wanted to spill the wind from the sails all I had to do was release the main sheet. With his faith in me and the reminder of what I'd been taught, I tried to relax into the boat's rhythm. Responsibility was heavy on my lap.

At our maximum speed of six knots, we traveled about one hundred miles in twenty-four hours. There was plenty of time to enjoy the stars.

The heavy life vest chafed against my chin and bare arms. I wriggled and itched, trying to find a comfortable position on the damp vinyl cushions. Giving up, I stretched out. The stars shimmered overhead, an ebony umbrella dotted in silver. The North Star, at the tip of the Big Dipper, made a good directional beacon. For the first time since stitching my Girl Scout badge to its green sash, I was conscious of the pattern in the sky. In my city life, the stars were washed out by street lights, neon signs and indifference. Here, the sky was my friend and I sensed why ancient mariners had named the stars after gods. I tried to count the stars but decided there must be billions. A big number.

The only sounds were the wind in the rigging, a buzz from the VHF radio and the sea rushing by our hull. The stars were hypnotizing and I thought back to the miracle of meeting Rick.

It was the first Saturday in December and I had hired a babysitter so I could go to a nightclub with a gal pal from work. By some divine plan or luck, Rick had gone to the same club. We were introduced, we talked, shared a light kiss and just two weeks later we sat in my living room on Christmas Eve. Although he was new in my life, we acted as though we'd been together forever.

It was the first Christmas since my divorce. My daughters were four and seven and excited that Santa Claus would come tonight. We had promised them we would make sure the fireplace was cold so that Santa wouldn't get hurt coming down the chimney. They eventually succumbed to the sleepy world of children anticipating Santa's arrival, and Rick and I arranged gifts under the tree, filled the stockings and made eggnogs for ourselves.

That Thanksgiving had been a nightmare. Lisa and Amy were with their father and his family while I dined on Cornish game hen for one. Nine years earlier I had pledged, in front of a hundred guests, "For better or worse." Failure caught like dry stuffing in my throat and I had shoved my solo plate across the kitchen table and tried to think of something to be thankful for. I had pulled a coloring book toward me and on the blank inside back cover, in bright red crayon, I started a list.

- healthy
- two wonderful little girls
- a job
- f

I had started to write "family" but stopped, sniffled and stabbed with my napkin at the tears spilling over. Neither my parents nor siblings had thought of how needy I might be today. They had left town on various vacations and I hadn't heard a word. The red "f" stared back at me.

Using a green crayon, I carefully wrote, "riends." But how many friends had called? None. I crossed it out.

I shook my head to dislodge the negativity my list was breeding. I turned the tablet over. Staring at the blank space, I slowly drew the shape of a cow; that's how attractive I felt. I'd always been a Pollyanna, so I sketched whimsical wings, like butterflies, on her back. At least I was smiling now.

In purple crayon I began a list of what would make me happy.
- Waking up laughing, going to sleep smiling.
- Sharing my ideas, listening to my partner's dreams.
- Touching, hugging.
- Parenting together and enjoying the company of my partner, who loves my daughters as much as I do.

That's what I wrote.

"*and maybe cows will fly*" I scrawled across the bottom of the page, thinking how unlikely it was that such a partner might come my way.

But he did. "Joy to the World" sang from the speakers in the corner while the fire between us crackled. Just four weeks earlier I had been lonely and sad. Then this man with a laugh that bubbled like champagne entered my life. He had eyes the color of mink and looked comfortable in my antique rocking chair. He had never spent a Christmas with children but his contented smile suggested that a sense of peace was settling over him.

We married and became a family. "My daughters" became "our girls." Rick brought humor and hugs into the house, showing by example the joy of being loved. He spoke to my heart without saying a word. We progressed from tricycles to prom dresses, putting salve on skinned knees and tending bruised teenage hearts. The daily grind of jobs, mortgages and busy lives layered over us and occasionally made us furious with each other but we treasured our love and took good care of it. The years slipped by and soon we were packing the girls off to college.

The kitchen timer I wore around my neck alerted me to my on-watch duties. Startled, I stared at the small black-and-white cow ornament that swung from *Nanook*'s railing. For a decade she had hung over our kitchen sink like mistletoe, reminding us that "Cows do fly."

I went below to check the radar and to mix a cup of raspberry hot chocolate. The chart indicated we would soon cross shipping lanes. In Navigation class I'd learned that a freighter travels from the horizon in less than twenty minutes. They rarely have anyone on watch and if they do we would be just a smudge on their radar screen despite the blipper we'd installed.

There's a frightful story that boaters tell about a freighter arriving in port with a large piece of canvas wrapped around its bow, the remnants of an inattentive sailor. On a dance floor as large as the ocean, the odds were in our favor but if we were going to avoid bumping toes with a freighter, it was up to me.

When my turn to sleep came and I traded places with Rick, I struggled out of my life vest and snuggled under the sheet on the lee settee. The swollen moon swayed, visible through the companionway opening. I savored the delicious feeling of cotton on my skin and burrowed into my cocoon for a few hours of sleep. My last thought as I watched the moon through the opening was that I was inept but certainly not bored. Sailing toward the horizon scared me but it was also challenging, not unlike raising babies into adults.

At daybreak, the coffee pot gurgled. Within fifteen minutes the cabin smelled of fresh coffee, a nautical love note. We filled our cups and sat in the cockpit sharing crusty French toast and sweet guava juice. A smear of red lipstick underscored a navy sky, separating it from the horizon. Like a giant hand lifting a lid, the sky lightened from the bottom up, revealing the promise of a clear day; a day that yawned blankly in front of us, unmarked by scheduled events.

Reclining on a sail bag, I studied a strip of white that wasn't big enough to be a cloud. It had the same shape as the tail of white foam that followed us. The sunlight caught a ripple for just a moment and diamonds danced across the water.

Having time for these kinds of musings was a first. We were used to long to-do lists crammed into busy work schedules. In a partial retreat to the familiar, I grabbed a yellow legal pad and composed a list of observations.

1. The ocean is enormous. If I was lost on land, I could ask directions or use maps and signs to navigate the urban grid. Out here there's no one to ask and no signs.
2. Everything familiar is behind us, on land, which I can't see.
3. Panic, or something like it, is poking her fingers into me and stirring madly.
4. I have time. Lots of it.

As the day progressed, the weather changed. The seas grew angry and a steady progression of agitated five-foot waves pounded the hull. *Nanook* bounced like a cork. I struggled to my feet but my timing was off. A bigger wave tossed us to port and I fell, catching myself on the automatic pilot contraption. I rubbed at the blood trickling down my leg. It was sobering to consider that in really bad weather we could die out here.

The weather class I'd taken had filled my brain with random knowledge. I stood next to Rick under the awning. We braced ourselves with feet spread wide and I raised my arms to grip the dodger's stainless steel supports. We looked out across whitecaps that stretched to infinity.

"A wave is pure energy. It's just water being pushed and dragged across the surface by the wind, tides and air pressure," I said, using my teacher voice. "Waves are born in deep water and as the depth of the ocean changes, like when the wave meets the shore, it dies on the beach." I was silenced by a blanket of whitewater that washed the bow.

"Is that all?" Rick asked.

"Yep. Class dismissed," I replied, leaning over to give him a salty kiss.

As dusk fell, the wind decreased and the seas flattened. The night was a skintight leotard blocking anything in front of us from view while plankton glowed like underwater fireflies, creating glittering ribbons of phosphorescence in our wake.

> *"Life is either a daring adventure or nothing."*
>
> HELEN KELLER

CHAPTER 5

Landfall

DAWN OF DAY three turned the sky off our stern a dozen shades of orange, illuminating the dark mass of *Isla Guadalupe*. We had traveled 202 miles from San Diego and the course Rick had charted found land. We raised our cups of vanilla nut coffee in a toast to our first landfall.

In the few minutes it took to be sure our anchor was holding, a *panga* motored across the bay and two smiling Mexicans appeared at our starboard rail. Their twenty-foot open boat was high in the bow with a duct-taped outboard motor rigged to the transom. The boat looked as if it had once been painted green but now it showed splatters of red that could have been fish blood or rust.

One of the men tossed a gunny sack of lobsters into our cockpit and gestured in pantomime. It seemed natural to barter so many miles from civilization so I went below and returned with an armload of canned peas,

Spam and warm beer. The two shoved off, waving and saying something in Spanish. It sounded like, "*Vamos a regresar,*" but I was foggy from lack of sleep and their voices drifted across the water. We waved goodbye.

Leaving the lobsters to crawl around the cockpit, Rick went to the bow to inflate the dinghy while I got out an omelet pan and began beating eggs. The rumble from an outboard motor signaled that we had visitors again. Rick called into the cabin, "Honey, those guys are back."

I turned the propane off and climbed into the cockpit. With a broad smile that showed gaps where teeth should have been, the man in the stern said, "*Me llamo Juan Pedro,*" pointing to himself, "*Es mi amigo, Antonio,*" gesturing to his partner in the bow. "*Vamos a pescar. Quisiera ir con nosotros?*"

Rick and I introduced ourselves and agreed with a nod and a hug that he would go fishing with them. He collected his gear while I slapped a sandwich together.

Climbing down the boarding ladder and into the *panga*, Rick stepped calf-deep into a jumble of fishing line. He looked at me with uncertainty. The three were heading out to sea. If the outboard quit they could float for months, away from the island and *Nanook*.

The red spiny lobsters crawled over each other, two deep, and one was heading toward the companionway stairs. I leapt to the top step and swatted the critter back into the pile with his crustacean pals. Pulling the largest enamel cast iron kettle from its storage space under the settee, I filled it with water and turned on the stove. Four of the wily guys used each other as stepping stones, getting closer to the stairs than made me comfortable. I slid a hatch board into the opening. These boards are designed to keep water out of the cabin in a storm. I was glad to see that they worked for lobsters, too.

I poured myself a glass of white wine thinking that it must be five o'clock somewhere. It was just 9:00 AM but my internal clock had no idea what time it was. Rick and I had been trading the on-watch duty for three days. I lifted my glass in the direction of the lobsters, offering a toast to our first landfall and the critters while I waited for the water to boil.

I hadn't bathed since we left San Diego, so I found my towel and shampoo and stripped out of my shorts and shirt. Hanging the towel over the life line, I started down the boarding ladder. Just as I put my right foot into the water, a shark about half the length of *Nanook* cruised toward me.

I jumped back into the cockpit while the beast slid under *Nanook*'s belly on the port side. It surfaced again on the starboard side. I watched the underwater stalker and shuddered, foolishly covering myself with the bath towel as if it were a person approaching. Its torpedo-shaped body and pointed snout made it look like a submarine. Its midsection was the size of a hula-hoop. I'd read that they have about 3,000 teeth arranged in several rows.

Bathing with my visitor wasn't an option, so I showered on the bow using a solar shower suspended from the rigging. I consoled myself with the lack of a bath by relishing the view from my improvised shower stall.

Rick returned from fishing and while he packed fresh grouper fillets in the ice box next to baggies filled with lobster meat, he told me about his day. It was our first day spent more than a few feet apart.

"The guys used chunks of raw lobster for bait. That seemed weird."

"I guess it makes sense to use what's here, but is what they're catching worth as much as the bait?" I asked.

"They use a chunk of lobster to catch grouper, which they use to bait the lobster traps."

"They've probably been at it for centuries."

We sat in the cockpit looking at *Isla Guadalupe* about 200 yards off our starboard side. Rock and undersea pinnacles surrounded it. Cinder cones dotted the landscape and lava caves and tubes guarded the shoreline. Water sucked into the caves, sounding like the brass section of an amateur orchestra warming up. The scent of low tide drifted on the air.

"I was worried about you," I continued. "What if the outboard had quit? How would you have gotten back? Did you think about that?"

"Oh, yeah. That was seriously on my mind but Juan and Tony have kids and wives on the island and they've been doing this forever."

"So Antonio became Tony? How could you understand each other? Your Spanish is worse than mine."

"We passed the dictionary back and forth. It's pretty amazing how much can be said in a single word. Especially "shark."

"What is the Spanish word for shark?"

"*El tiburon. Senor Tiburon* for respect," Rick laughed.

I told him about my aborted bath. He nodded in agreement. "We won't do any swimming here, I guess. I saw 'em, too. I felt really vulnerable, too, floating out there in a bucket the size of a gravy boat. But lunch was great," he continued.

"Peanut butter without jam? What was great about that?"

"I traded the PB on wheat for their grilled lobster on fresh tortillas. That made it a two for one as far as I was concerned."

I laughed, thinking that our canned peas for lobster swap seemed too good to be true, too.

Easy swells rolled *Nanook* like a swinging hammock. We moved to the bow where I stretched out on the cabin roof and Rick sat on the staysail bag.

He told me that his compadres didn't use fishing poles. Instead, they wrapped their line from the snarled mess on the floor of the boat around some worn notebook-sized boards. They tied pipe wrenches and spark plugs to the line as weights. By contrast, Rick's rod and reel still had the price tags attached.

He went on to describe a day punctuated by forty- to fifty-pound tuna, four feet long, leaping out of the ocean. Shaped like overinflated supersized footballs, they had launched themselves as if tossed by a pro quarterback. "There were so many and they were so fast it was a blur."

Fish knocked on the hull while we chatted on the bow. Our cruising guide said that the great white sharks congregate at *Isla Guadalupe* to feed on the sea lions, and judging from the noise level on shore there was plenty of food left.

The next morning we dropped the dinghy in the water and attached the outboard motor. According to our chart, a settlement of abalone and lobster fishermen, called *Campo Oeste,* was on the west coast of the island and we needed permission to go ashore. *Guadalupe* is a volcanic island, just twenty-two miles long and about five miles wide. We motored along the coastline looking for the best place to land a small rubber boat.

At the southern tip, Melpómene Cove, we came to a weather station that our book said was staffed by a detachment from the Mexican Ministry of the Navy. Near the stairs, a large man, shirtless and in ragged tan shorts sat on a rock with a fishing pole in his hands. As we approached, he was so still, I thought he was asleep.

"*Hola, discúlpame,*" I called softly. He bobbed his pole at us, nodding that he knew we were there. Rick steered the dinghy close and the man pointed for us to tie up near the rock next to the one he was using as a chair. I leaned over the bow and tied the dinghy.

"*Podríamos desembarcar? Permiso del Capitan del Puerto?*" Our guidebook had led us to believe that there was a complicated procedure for gaining access to the island. The man chuckled and said, "*Se fue de pescar,*" poking his own chest.

Apparently, he was the Port Captain and he'd gone fishing. Since he was so friendly, I asked him the purpose for the Navy's presence on the island. He said, "*Protegemos la patria.*" I looked it up in the Spanish dictionary I carried in my pocket. He had said, "We protect the mainland."

An image of the Navy Seals and the USS *Kitty Hawk* we'd sailed past a week earlier came to mind. From what I could see of Isla Guadalupe, a military encampment armed with fishing poles might not be prepared to fend off an attack from anything bigger than our small sailboat. We nodded respectfully and walked away, waving our thanks.

Picking our way up a steep path, we matched the strides cut by decades of goats and whatever else had tramped in the same narrow ruts. Through the window of an adobe church on the hilltop we saw *Nanook* at anchor. She looked like a child's crayon drawing from this distance. The only sounds were the wind over the rocks and the "clack clacking" of a dozen albatross waddling in mated pairs. They sounded like high-pitched rattling chains and looked like overgrown seagulls with black and gray brush strokes across their backsides. The ungainly birds were about three feet long, weighing five to ten pounds. Their six-foot wingspans gave an otherworldly aura to the desolate landscape of dust and scrub brush.

A cypress forest at the island's north end is home to the Cooperative Farming Society. Generators provided electricity and the men we saw told us that a military ship delivered fresh water and supplies every thirty days. Between deliveries, they bartered with each other, as the men in the *panga* had with us.

Retracing our steps, we returned to the landing. The dinghy was gone.

"Oh my God, where is it?" I cried.

Rick scanned the cove and said, "Over there."

The dinghy was about two hundred yards away. We scrambled over rocks along the water's edge and Rick swam out to it.

The knot I'd tied had slipped off. I had failed the

marlinespike seamanship class where they taught knot tying, which was obvious now. Rick was good at it but he wouldn't always be the one handling the lines. We'd been lucky this time but didn't want to count on luck. Back on *Nanook*, Rick braided a snap shackle to the end of the line.

While we were involved in a crisis we worked as a team. It was afterward that we aimed poison darts at each other.

"I'm so sorry, that was careless. Oh honey, tell me you're not mad," I pleaded.

Rick didn't look up. He lit a match to burn the ends of the nylon to keep the line from unraveling and pressed it into shape.

"Say something, honey," I continued.

"I'd rather not until I calm down."

"You're mad, I can tell. But it was an accident."

"Christie, don't push. You made a mistake and we can't make mistakes out here."

I'm easily shattered and started to cry but Rick wasn't in the mood. He left me alone with my guilt and went below to read a book.

By morning we had put the argument away.

We rocked at anchor in the sunshine for a week. Schools of tuna swam by. The occasional shark showed his back. I baked my first loaf of bread.

The waters surrounding *Isla Guadalupe* are clear with visibility to about one hundred feet. We saw bluefin and yellowfin tuna and strange-looking gelatin plankton. Garibaldi, parrotfish, triggerfish and butterfly fish swam in the aquarium below us. We saw seals and bottlenose dolphins but the obvious presence of sharks kept us out of the water.

We ate lobster and grouper for breakfast, lunch and dinner. On our last night, I hummed with Jimmy Buffett. *"Islands, I see you in the distance, dah dah dah, just makes me want that much more."*

The vanishing sun spilled a crimson path over the water. Stars glowed like a million tiny porch lights and a diamond-studded path rippled across the water.

We were up early, watching the stars fade into an early morning sky. In the dim light, Rick lashed the dinghy face down on the bow. I closed the port holes, bungeed the cabin lantern to keep it from swinging and made sure that everything breakable was stowed firmly where it belonged. We plotted a southeasterly course toward the Baja and at dawn Rick hauled the anchor on board.

We wanted to simulate sailing off the anchor as a practice drill in case our motor wouldn't start, so before starting the motor, Rick hoisted the sail while I held the tiller. We were an awkward team at the unfamiliar drill but since the motor was working we figured we had time to practice.

Leaving the protection of the 4,000-foot cliffs of *Guadalupe*, the seas grew to ten feet and the wind hovered at twenty-five knots. The morning turned dark. In a house or an office, the muffled sounds and softened edges of a leaden day had been comforting. At sea, the dark sky was mirrored in the water and the resulting gray on gray had the warmth of a prison yard.

I stir-fried slices of lobster meat with a can of chow mein noodles for lunch. We took shifts of four hours on duty and four hours off. Our underway routine resumed. Eat, sleep, steer. Repeat.

The seas were sloppy and the wind continued to pound us from the stern. The boom and jib rigging slammed with the vigor of a teenage drummer. It was sobering to consider that we would be underway regardless of the conditions.

Rick tied a fishing line to a shock cord and slipped it over a stern cleat so we could fish. We also trailed a line from a fishing pole slipped in a holder on the aft rail.

When the shock cord jumped, I saw a fish the color of olive oil leap from the sea. We'd dined on delicious grouper fillets, had lobster omelets, lobster stew, lobster cocktails and lobster stir fry but now the ice box was empty. I put on thick rubber gloves and hand over hand, hauled in a 44-inch dorado, a "mahi-mahi."

It filled the cockpit. We'd have sushi. Any sailor worth her sea salt had a pantry stocked with wasabi, soy sauce and cabbage and I wrote menus in my head. Rick butchered and filleted and the self-steering kept us on course. While Rick rinsed fish guts from our living room by throwing buckets of sea water on the mess, I packaged the fillets in bundles and put them on what was left of our block of ice. Tomorrow Rick would grill, I'd fry and we'd pickle the rest.

A zzzzing from the fishing line on the pole interrupted us. In the excitement, we'd forgotten to reel in the other line. It was a breakfast-size *charrito*, a Pacific jack mackerel.

> *"I read and walked for miles at night along the beach, writing bad blank verse and searching endlessly for someone wonderful who would step out of the darkness and change my life. It never crossed my mind that the person could be me."*
>
> ANNA QUINDLEN

CHAPTER 6
Scribbles

ON MY FORTY-SEVENTH birthday, I splashed on the bow in my birthday suit. Rick had inflated our four-foot purple-and-yellow-striped child's swimming pool and I reclined in the salty suds.

I had just put shampoo in my hair when a "whooshing" sound came from our port side. We were sailing wing-and-wing with the jib poled to starboard and the main stretched on the port, so my view was blocked by the sails. Then it came again. Now it sounded like the hiss of a sizzling tea kettle. The diesel was running to charge the batteries and Rick looked over the railing to see if anything strange was belching from the exhaust. He shook his head.

I stood up and bubbles clung like polka dots to my body.

"Nice suit!" Rick called out.

I laughed and pretended to cover my body with my

hands but the hissing and splashing grew louder and I stepped out of the makeshift tub.

"There. Look," I said, pointing. Geysers went up and down like a calliope. There were at least thirty of them less than fifty yards away. Whales. Our first sighting.

Rick dropped the main and I hurriedly rinsed the shampoo from my hair. Rick furled the jib and we bobbed at sea for an hour watching the whales spout and dive.

"That was quite a show. Can I assume you planned it for my birthday?" I joked.

"But of course, milady. Nothing but the finest for *Nanook*'s First Mate," Rick replied with a deep bow and sweeping arm before returning his attention to sailing.

I went below to get dressed. On my way back to the cockpit, I plucked the red leather journal from a row of colorful spines on the shelf. It had been a goodbye gift from the English department.

Stretched out on top of the inflated dinghy, I was prone on the bow with the journal and pen in hand. I thought about the changes in my life. An image of myself as a young girl drifted by. I was about ten, lying on my back in green grass, naming the puffy clouds and making up vivid tales. I didn't actually write the stories but I told them to myself.

My fascination with words grew in Sunday school. The Biblical passages were poetic and I was entranced. My family teased that I really loved words. Grade school teachers often wrote on my report card, "Christie talks too much."

My fascination with the melodic nature of language never waned. I studied English literature in college and became a teacher. I thought my love of words would expand to writing but it didn't. For the next decades I helped our girls with homework, folded laundry and drove carpools. It had never occurred to me to keep a journal.

I sat up and rolled the cool barrel of the pen in my right hand. Peering at a streak of white clouds stretching across the sky, I wondered if the passage of time had acted like a vacuum cleaner and sucked up my words.

I'd been distracted for a few decades. Who had I been before I was Mom? Was I a child who lived for the moment? In my teens, did I gobble up life like a big bowl of spaghetti? The answer was "No." My concern had been about tomato stains on a white blouse with a Peter Pan collar. I shunned messes, mistakes and their bigger partner, failure.

Was it too late to become a woman who could get sticky and enjoy the cinnamon on my fingers without needing to wash? The search for perfection hadn't been a friendly partner and I longed to shed her.

I squinted at the clouds dancing overhead. My old companion, self-doubt, sat next to me. The blank journal pages taunted that I wasn't capable of worthwhile thoughts or lively descriptions.

I argued with the negative bully. If I failed, did it matter? I had been, at best, an average teacher. If it turned out that I was no more than an average writer, at least I would be average at something I yearned to do. I felt the boat lift and glide through the water, along with the shining touch of an idea.

I shoved self-doubt overboard and started scribbling.

> I am not a woman who likes sharp, jagged edges of change. "Wife" and "mother" are the roles that have defined me. Given my life meaning. The schedules and plans of Rick, Lisa and AJ have defined the shape of my days. Structure and family have been my anchors. I've been a spider on an obsessively organized web but I no longer want to maintain the pattern.
>
> I'm closer to 50 than 40, trimming the sails of a 37-foot sailboat off the west coast of the Baja of Mexico. Living at sea without my ordered land life, will I, figuratively as well as literally, float out to sea, a ship without a home port?

The magnitude of the thought startled me and I put down my pen. What does a mother do when her daughters leave for college and her husband wants an adventure? I realized I had lots to write about.

I kept scribbling.

> We've pulled up our collective stakes with only the slimmest notion of how we'll paddle into the future. Years ago we took a different, but no less significant, plunge when we stood before family

and friends and vowed "for better or worse, in sickness and in health."

I've always steered the safe route, down the middle of the road where surprises can't grab me. But my partnership with Rick has been full of surprises. He's certain that answers to today's puzzles lie just around the next bend. He searches for adventure while I wait in the wings and peer around the corner. Rick gets goofy with anticipation at the idea of being in unknown places and plowing through uncharted waters. Maybe that's how he found the courage to marry a newly divorced woman with two young daughters. Given his lack of cold feet at that important time, I'm not questioning his eager approach now. So we're sailing into our unknown future.

A FEELING OF DELIGHT

With utter astonishment
I watch the moon
lift from the horizon.
I have no agenda
and rock to the rhythm
of the sea.
I taste the air and
lick the breeze.
Like a purple kite
I soar.
I am part of
wind, water and whales.

> "Time is the coin of your life. It is the only coin you have and only you can determine how it will be spent. Be careful lest you let other people spend it for you."
>
> CARL SANDBURG

CHAPTER 7

Cruising

DUSK PULLED ITS shade and I began my on-watch shift with the safety harness snapped to the cockpit sole. The seas were too rough for the autopilot so I disabled it and hand steered. I caressed the smooth wood of the tiller with my thumb, cradling its shaft gently in my palm.

Our bow rode the sea in a rhythmic bucking motion that sent spray into my hair and crusted my bare arms. I licked my lips to taste the salt; *Nanook* moaned like a woman in the throes of passion.

After only an hour Rick's sleepy face appeared at the stairs. His hair stood on end and a pillow seam creased his left cheek. He was smiling. I smiled back.

"You're early," I said.

He wrapped his arms around me and said "And you're salty. Get some rest. I love you."

We traded on-watch duty every two hours until the

seas flattened and the autopilot could do her job. We finished the night with a three-hour on-watch cycle.

At dawn, I crawled out of bed and shuffled the few steps to the galley and flipped on the propane, igniting the fire under the coffee pot. Sticking my head into the cockpit, I saw Rick, pencil in hand, engrossed in a yellow legal pad. When I asked what he was doing, he looked up as if I'd broken a spell.

"Planning my sales meeting," he mumbled.

"Well, look in the mirror, sweetie, you're all that's left of your sales team."

Rick chuckled, well aware that the tasks he was listing he would do himself:
- Check the clasp on the port cockpit locker
- Find a better place to store the storm drogue
- Test the spinnaker
- Pour vinegar in the head

The habit of running a weekly sales meeting was going to take time to abate. As our time at sea lengthened, Rick internalized that he wasn't on vacation, that this was permanent, at least for now.

With steaming mugs of coffee cupped in our hands we watched the faint outline on the horizon articulate into details. Shades of green multiplied into trees, bushes and branches. We motor-sailed into the lee of an outcropping of rocks and dropped anchor. Palm trees lined the beach like frosting on a birthday cake.

We'd never done a beach landing through surf in the dinghy but I knew the time had to come someday. Going to shore we rode the crest of a wave and landed inelegantly but intact on the sand. Getting back through the surf wouldn't be as easy.

After exploring the island, we walked the dinghy into the water. "I can't," I said when Rick explained our maneuver.

He climbed in and rowed, pointing us straight into the surf. I grabbed the transom, pushed and leapt through the waves. Rick watched the incoming waves over his shoulder. When he yelled "Now!" I rolled over the rubber pontoon onto the floor of the dinghy and a wave crashed over us. I sat up coughing and laughing through a mouthful of salt water. Rick rowed with fury while I yanked the starter cord. It roared to life and we shot through the next wave. Rick shoved the oars in their locks and we howled at the mess we'd made of our maiden launch. At least no one was on shore to witness the clumsiness.

We explored the whaling village at Belcher's Cove and celebrated Thanksgiving with the three other boats in the bay. The eight of us tossed towels on the gravel beach and ate clams instead of turkey. After three days we sailed south to *Cabo San Lucas*.

The waves in the *Cabo* anchorage pitched us bow to stern like a bucking bronco. Despite the hobby horse conditions, we loaded the dinghy with dirty clothes and our check-in paperwork. Rick climbed in and saw a repair he could do. He tugged on the dinghy's valve to add air to the starboard pontoon but the apparatus came off in his hand, sucking it inside the tube. Rick was trying the maneuver for the first time, in deep water and with the outboard attached. Okay, it was a lousy idea, but this wasn't the time to discuss a better one. A gaping two-inch hole was sinking the dinghy, the motor, and its contents.

Rick sprang into action, launching our gear at *Nanook* with the velocity of an airport luggage handler at a conveyor belt fire. He tossed an oar, then the foot pump, the briefcase and the laundry bag. The inflatable deflated and gurgled underwater.

Jumping back on board, he was tugging on the bow line when I took a turn at poor strategizing. Dressed to go to town in a gauzy broomstick skirt, shrimp pink scoop-neck top and seashell necklace, I hopped onto *Nanook*'s railing, grabbed the dinghy's bridle and leapt into the water. My plan was to clip the snap shackle to the block and tackle, Rick would crank it up and the outboard would stay dry. At least that's what I pictured in haste. It might have been a good idea except that I forgot to untie the line before I leapt.

The scene would have made a good pilot show under the title *Laurel and Hardy Arrive in Cabo* but we weren't seeing the humor.

I swam back to *Nanook*. Rick looked at me as if I'd lost my mind. "Kind of an odd time for a swan dive don't ya' think?" his look said. Fortunately, he was absolutely silent.

We dragged the flooded dinghy on board. Rick glued

the gasket back in place and inflated the pontoons. We hired someone to flush the salt water from the outboard. More than a few hours later we went to shore, checked in with the port authorities and did the laundry.

On departure day from *Cabo* I wrote in my journal.

> Coffee's brewing, toast is on its rack over the propane burner and I'm watching a raspberry jam sunrise spread itself across the ocean. We were anchor up and stern to the harbor at 0715. Cabo made me sad. Everywhere we were faced with Americans wanting American food, currency, service and language; they should have stayed home. A booby bird is hitchhiking on our radar. Smart bird. Like me, he wants to escape Cabo and its frenetic tourism.

We were finishing a breakfast of chorizo and eggs when the fishing shock cord jerked tight with a simultaneous splash twenty feet behind us. We shoved our breakfast plates aside and I untied the gaff hook. Rick put on gloves and, hand over hand, hauled a yellow and pink dorado on board.

Some people fillet fish, but small motor skills aren't Rick's strong suit, so butchering was a more accurate description. The result was a dozen steaks and a mountain of shavings. I tucked the baggies of meat around a block of ice and returned to the cockpit.

Rick hollered, "Fish on."

"Very funny," I retorted. The cockpit was still slimy with blood and fish guts and we didn't have any space in the icebox. I looked aft and sure enough, another large fish was slicing the sea like a scalpel. Before either of us could put on gloves, the line flew in the air and the fish spit out the hook. Rick coiled the slack line, not wanting to risk catching more fish than we could use.

Usually the wind died when the sun went down but tonight it picked up speed and the waves grew taller. Rick went forward to lash the water jugs to the stanchions. When he returned, we huddled under the dodger, gripping the rails so we could stand upright while *Nanook* heeled hard to starboard. The wind screamed, making conversation impossible even though we were side by side. After about an hour, Rick hollered, "Can't wait any longer, gotta reduce the main. Steer us into the wind."

I stepped out of the lee of the dodger and yanked the self-steering bracket off the tiller while Rick went forward. I steered us into the wind, spilling the sail's power and Rick disappeared into the ink-black night. Long nightmarish minutes dragged by.

I screamed, "Are you okay?"

The wind howled through the rigging. The luffing sail popped like gunfire. I hoped Rick had snapped his harness to the mast but I couldn't see anything in the black night.

"Rick, Rick, answer me."

Only the wind answered with an unrelenting howl.

I wrestled with the tiller and prayed that Rick was

snap-shackled to the mast, not bobbing like a coconut in an ocean the color of tar.

My mouth was open to scream again when Rick thumped into the cockpit.

"Thank God" escaped my lips.

"Whew, it's bad out there," Rick said with a calm that made no sense to me. He took the tiller from my clenched fist and re-attached the self-steering. Steady as a lighthouse beacon, he stood at the helm. Standing next to him, I felt my tension ebb.

I turned and reached for his face with both hands and kissed him. Lips, jawline, eyes, nose, eyebrows and ears. He was covered in delicious salt spray and I was washed by surging relief.

"Great greeting," he said when I released him from my grasp. "What was that for?"

"I was so scared. Scared you didn't snap-on to the boat. Terrified you'd fallen overboard." I burst into tears.

Two full days later we approached Marina *Mazatlan* as the sun was low in the sky. We were losing the battle against the setting sun and I felt a powerful urge to reach out and lift it just another foot off the horizon to buy us an hour of daylight. Entering an unfamiliar port in the dark was risky but we didn't want to spend another night at sea.

"Sure would be nice to go fast," Rick said.

"Four knots is about average isn't it?" I asked.

"Well, yes, but I really miss speed. Maybe it's all those

years in the car business. If this thing had a gas pedal I'd floor it and we'd be at the dock in five minutes."

Instead, we entered the breakwater after dusk, straining to see.

Being in the marina meant sleeping together in the V-berth again, a welcome change after a passage. In the morning we found out that we didn't need to check-in with *Mazatlan* immigration; the paperwork was handled for us by the marina.

There was a pig roast and we met new friends. We stayed for three weeks, exploring *Mazatlan*'s French colonial old town and eating ribs at a popular "all you can eat" palapa. In the hot afternoons we sat in the shade and played pig mania and Mexican train dominoes. Sometimes we played golf and other days we scrounged the port district for marine hardware stores.

The cruiser net announced a marina provisions swap. Ladies cleaned out their cupboards and men rifled their tool boxes. I traded three cans of tomato paste, a dented can of peas, a box of raisin bran and two cans of turkey chili for someone's French vanilla coffee, shrimp paté, amaretto crackers and lemon pepper croutons. A good deal for me, I thought.

While we were in port, I made a stab at being Mom, but an occasional phone call couldn't be called a relationship. Besides, my new life so captivated me that I had few emotional reserves left over.

When I found a pay phone that worked and if I had coins or a local phone card, I dialed the girls' numbers.

But my timing was based on my life, not theirs, and most of the time I just left a message. Of course, there was no way they could return the call. I wrote letters but our stars didn't align very often.

My calls to Lisa left me tugging at my right to be away. She was floundering her way into the adult world and in the process was spending more money than we'd budgeted. All I could do was hope she would live on a no-frills budget, which might have been too much to ask.

> "You really live by the water? What a jolly life!"
> "By it and with it and on it and in it," said the Rat.
> "It's my world and I don't want any other.
> What it hasn't got is not worth having
> and what it doesn't know is not worth knowing.
> Lord, the times we've had...."
>
> KENNETH GRAHAME,
THE WIND IN THE WILLOWS

CHAPTER 8
Life at Sea

WE LIVED WITHOUT refrigeration, bled air from the engine lines in dark rough seas and entertained landlubber house guests while bouncing at anchor. But getting used to our new lives was anything but a seamless progression. I'd always made plans. I'd set and met deadlines. Now I was discarding plans and going on feel.

One of our earliest live-aboard lessons on *Nanook* was "doing the dance." That's what Rick called our choreography. There simply wasn't room for two adults to clear the table, put things away, or head for the stairs at the same time. It took some getting used to, as did other aspects of live-aboard life.

A Crealock is designed for ocean sailing so *Nanook* rode low in the water. The tangible result was that we didn't have an aft stateroom. Visiting other boats, I realized that most of our friends had a choice at the foot of

the stairs, they could go aft into another room or forward to the cabin. I developed a severe case of stair envy. We had one choice, forward.

Nanook's interior was a cozy haven that sane folks would call cramped. Her overall outside length was a long putt to a golfer but inside the cabin we were less than one-third of that. Rick and I slept in the bow's V-berth, our shoulders far apart with toes touching.

Our bathroom, the head, was so tiny that a single cotton-braided placemat fit like wall-to-wall carpeting with the fringe going slightly up the walls. We showered on deck with a solar shower and flushed the toilet with a long handle like the lever of a slot machine. To keep the plumbing hoses clear, we poured vinegar in the bowl to dissolve the salt build-up that turned the insides of the hoses to cement. Sometimes we removed the hoses

and jumped up and down on them on a dock to break up the residue.

In my land life, if we had fewer than a dozen rolls of toilet paper in the pantry, I'd have put "TP" on the shopping list. On *Nanook*, even when a *tienda* was in sight of the beach, we just used fewer squares. I marveled at how quickly I changed from stocking up to getting by with what we already had. It was an interesting transition that could destroy American big box store shopping, if it caught on.

When a small sailboat is a permanent home, finding storage space for everyday items is a challenge. Rick had a tendency to put tools, cups and bowls wherever he found space for them, not necessarily in the slot they came from. It drove me nuts. My obsession with order was equally annoying. At one point, I made a list of what was in every locker and tacked each sheet to the lid of the cupboard. To keep it current, I had a system that required every item we used to be crossed off and anything added would be written in. My plan not only didn't work, it was another reason we fought. The lists were tossed; I think we threw them at each other. We regressed to the search method.

While we were still on land, I designed canvas storage panels for the walls of the sleeping berths. We called them our "bunk buddies." The large pockets held tissues, journals and pens, books, magazines, flashlights and laundry. One pocket on each side functioned as the proverbial "junk drawer."

Our daily lives didn't include mail, a telephone, cars or television. Mail was forwarded in bundles by a service in Seattle and we communicated on the VHF and Ham radios. We used electricity conservatively. Our supply came from batteries charged by solar panels and we ran the engine with a high output alternator.

My exercise routine was a series of stretches on the bow and raising my arms in arcs holding a twenty-ounce chili can in each hand. Rick did deep knee bends wearing his scuba weight belt. We practiced our Spanish with flash cards.

Nanook held ninety gallons of fresh water. When we were near a village, we bought five-liter jugs, lugged them to the dinghy and motored out to the boat. Connecting a siphon and balancing the water jug higher than the opening created a gravity flow to fill the tanks. We conserved water by washing dishes in a bucket of salt water in the cockpit and rinsing with fresh water in the sink. We used about two gallons of fresh water a day.

We didn't have a water pressure system, which helped us to conserve. A foot pump below each sink produced a steady stream of unheated water. On a visit to see the girls, I stood in a fully equipped bathroom, stomping my foot like Walt Disney's Thumper. I'd forgotten about faucets.

When we were in port, we took laundry to a *lavanderia*. Underway, we let the boat's motion slosh wet clothes in a large bucket and rinsed them in the inflatable bathtub. Rick twisted the shirts and shorts dry and I clipped them to the lifelines.

In the center of *Nanook*'s cabin was a folding mahogany dining table. Opened, it could seat six. Twin settees upholstered in soft caramel tweed were accented with bright turquoise and green throw pillows. The settees did triple duty as dining room chairs, short sofas and they became our beds when we were underway.

Above the settees on both sides were shelves filled with books and movie tapes. A removable railing kept them from spilling out when the boat heeled. A bungee cord tethered a nine-inch television with a built-in tape player. It operated on twelve-volt power so we could watch movies without being in a marina. We swapped tapes with other boaters for variety.

Hammocks hung from teak handrails and bulged with perishable foods. Bread, crackers and tortillas swayed on the port side. Suspended in the starboard hammock an array of fresh fruit and vegetables swung to the rhythm of the sea. Using overhead space was prudent in cramped quarters, but allowing fragile goods to swing freely also kept them from getting bruised or crushed.

The galley cupboards held plastic dishes and wine glasses, bread baking pans, coffee mugs, spices and the canned goods that needed to be easily accessible. Lockers under the sofa cushions were filled with food staples. Extra cans of soup, stews, meats, vegetables and fruit fit tightly between zip-locked bags of sugar and flour.

Lockers under our mattresses in the bow held our wardrobes of T-shirts and shorts. A set of placemats and cloth napkins, a dictionary, CDs and a bit of needlepoint were tucked away, too. In a less accessible cupboard was a set of nesting bowls, the largest for potlucks.

We buddy boated the first few months with Steve and Naila on their Columbia 50, *Querida II*. Naila loved to sew but hadn't brought along a sewing machine and fabrics. Steve had convinced her that she could do without or buy what she needed in Mexico. Without her favorite activity, she grew restless and they quit cruising early. I was glad that Rick and I had not only loaded the boat with the gear we thought was necessary but also with the extra goodies that made it as home-like as possible.

The three-burner propane stove and oven were gimbaled to swing with the boat's movement. Underway, I used a pressure cooker because the lid clamped shut and rails around the stove made it possible to clamp the pots to the burners in rough seas. Hot water was heated on the stove.

Although most boats have refrigeration, we didn't. It had seemed like a luxury and an unnecessary expense when we were getting ready to go. Rick had theorized that if he couldn't repair it we probably shouldn't have it. Taking that logic to the next level, we probably wouldn't have gone cruising at all because "repair" was not his forte.

We kept cold food in an ice box built into the galley counter when ice was available. If we caught a large fish and didn't have ice we invited everyone within radio range to dine in our cockpit. Cold food was a rare treat and when ice was available we savored the taste of chilled drinks and the possibility of leftovers.

I used handy camping tricks to deal with the lack of refrigeration. I bought cabbage instead of lettuce and tore the leaves to avoid the spoilage caused by a knife. I learned that jam, ketchup and even mayonnaise don't need to be refrigerated as long as the spoon was completely clean with each insertion. I aged chunks of cheddar cheese in a plastic wide-mouth jar full of olive oil.

I stored the egg cartons in a hammock. In a class called "The Offshore Cook," I had learned to keep eggs fresh by turning the carton over every few days. This rotated the air pocket that leads to spoiling. I felt so smart with that bit of information that I tried to ignore my inability to tie sailor's knots in favor of focusing on food lessons. Before using an egg I gave each the float test in a bowl of water. Spoiled eggs float. In all our years on *Nanook* I only tossed a few bad eggs into the sea.

Tucked under the stairs next to the galley was our "go

bag," a waterproof package of emergency gear. It would be the first thing to grab if we hit a reef, a freighter or a whale and needed to abandon ship. The rule is that you stay with your boat as long as possible, but if she was sinking, we could grab the bag and get in the dinghy, since we didn't have a life raft. The "go bag" was filled with canned food, a small water maker, fishing tackle, a handheld GPS, portable VHF radio and an EPIRB, a device that sends a distress signal. We'd done all the drills and talked through our routines but prayed that we'd wasted the money.

Across from the galley and next to the stairs was the nav station. Mounted there was our GPS, radar, VHF and Ham radios and CD player. The top of the desk lifted on hinges for storage of charts and plotting graphs.

We used the VHF radio to talk to boats in close range, and busy marinas and anchorages had a daily "Morning Net" to share news and to answer local questions. It was light-hearted and casual but as important to cruisers as a staff meeting had been in our working lives. Every morning, when the Net ended, we hailed each other on the commonly listened-to frequency. It went something like this…

Nanook: Snow Goose, Snow Goose, this is *Nanook*.

Snow Goose: Nanook, this is *Snow Goose*. Six nine?

Nanook and *Snow Goose* turn their radio dials to Channel 69 and so does everyone else within range if they want to know what Christie and Molly have to say, or if they want to break in and talk to either of us.

Snow Goose: Nanook, this is *Snow Goose*. Over.

Nanook: *Hola*, Molly. Rick and I were excited to hear you and Bill check-in this morning. Did you guys just get here? Over.

Snow Goose: We dropped the hook last night. We're about 300 yards behind you. Over.

Nanook: We wanna hear about your trip. How about potluck on *Nanook*? Is 5 o'clock good? Over.

Snow Goose: Let me check with Bill. He's putting the dinghy in right now. We need to check in, get supplies. You know the drill. We'll knock on your hull to confirm in about an hour. OK? Over.

Nanook: We'll be here. Over.

Snow Goose, Snow Goose, this is *Silhouette*.

Nanook, Nanook, this is *Unicorn*.

If the VHF served as a telephone for local calls, the Single Side Band was for longer distance. SSB Nets were businesslike. Boats checked-in at specific times, giving their location and a weather report. For boaters far from shore it was a safety feature.

When we were at sea and needed to make a phone call, I could check in to a SSB Net using my Ham license, saying, "This is *Nanook*. XE2, Kilo, Charlie, seven, Hotel, Kilo, Whiskey with traffic." "Traffic" meant I wanted to talk to someone and I waited until the volunteer running the Net said it was my turn. We would be connected with a Ham radio operator in the States who would do a phone patch, dialing the call for us. Sometimes I volunteered to run one of the nets. At the appointed time

I sat at the nav station with my notes spread across the chart table like a cheat-sheet.

The rear quarter berth, a combination closet and garage, was behind the nav station. Anything and everything that didn't fit somewhere else got shoved there. Including our golf clubs. Every few months, we put the junior size bags in the dinghy and rode a bus to a local golf course. Once there, we were on familiar footing. Doing something we were good at delivered a dose of confidence while we figured out the nuances of sailing.

Nanook's three fuel tanks held 110 gallons of diesel. We filled them by taking the empties on a bus to the nearest town and returning in a taxi. Open fuel containers weren't allowed on the bus and they were too heavy to carry. When we were in a marina we had the luxury of pulling up to a fuel dock but that was rare.

Our nine-foot inflatable dinghy and outboard motor did double duty as car and life raft. Rick had mounted wheels on the transom so we could drag it above the surf line when we went ashore. At anchor, we used a bridle to suspend it above the water. This kept barnacles from growing on the hull in the warm water and worked as an effective theft deterrent. It also couldn't float away if I failed to secure it properly.

A gimbaled barbecue hung from a bracket mounted on the aft rail next to our flying cow talisman. A barbecue had seemed like a great idea when we were outfitting *Nanook*. We thought we would grill fresh fish and chicken or pork from the markets. In reality, we seldom used it because the wind was either blowing into the cockpit, the seas too rough, or Rick had recently dropped an important piece of it into the sea and we hadn't found a replacement yet.

Underway, we took turns being on watch and sleeping. A routine of sorts emerged. I changed the sheets while Rick changed the oil. I cooked the meals and Rick did the dishes. And so it went, each day following the next like elephants on a march, linked trunk to tail.

Nanook carved a path that sang through the sea and after a few months of ocean sailing we noticed that even a minor wind shift played a different tune. Writers who pen eloquent prose about the silence of the sea must be writing from desks on land. The rigging squawked and waves slapped. Shrimp sucked the hull, making a crunching noise that sounded like a giant walking on crackers. With only a pillow between my ear and the fiberglass hull, when I heard baritone reverberations, I dreamed it was whales singing, or the return of the dolphins. But it might have been a passing shrimper or freighter.

It wasn't lonely. We had each other, the radio, dolphins and stars for company. We saw whales, turtles and marlin. Booby birds used our railings and radar as landing platforms. After one thirty-two hour passage, I wrote in my journal.

> In my land life, nature was a backdrop. Now I'm immersed. This world that we have chosen – with no human beings as far as the eye can see, for days and days – shows so evidently the hand of

our Creator. The power of the dolphin, the mighty whale and purple sunsets. We float over patterns beyond the wildest imaginings of Picasso.

Rick took off his sunglasses and raised the binoculars. I put down my pen and shielded my eyes. I squinted into the glare to see what had captured his attention. I didn't see anything.

"I think it's just another crate. Here," he said, lifting the binocular strap from his neck and handing it to me.

I shook my head. I didn't need to see it. "How can you say, just another crate?" I asked, slipping the binoculars back in their teak rack. I'd read in a cruising magazine that containers fell off ships at an alarming rate. I pictured all the household goods of someone moving overseas gurgling to the bottom of the ocean. We had parted with our belongings on purpose, now I felt the horror of the owner who would never receive the lovingly packed contents. I picked up the binoculars and watched until it disappeared.

The perpetual motion of my land life was behind me. On *Nanook,* I had no power to make us go faster and no reason to be in a hurry. Brisk day sails, the kind you see from the shore on a Sunday afternoon, is not how liveaboards sail. Cruisers are headed to a specific destination, while a day sailor picks a direction based on the wind. Day sailors want to heel sharply, burying the rail. A cruising boat is heavy and doesn't dance on the water.

The absence of speed gave the sensation that time

was infinite. I stood on the bow, my arms spread wide, embracing all the shades of blue that only changed in intensity, uninterrupted by contrasting colors. The air smelled of salt and diesel. The rumbling engine was as much a part of me as my own heartbeat.

I shaded my eyes from the glare and squinted at a commotion in the distance. It looked like about a hundred dolphins off our port side. I'd grown accustomed to their shows and I smiled at the sight. They might come closer and play with our bow, entertaining for minutes or an hour or they might turn tail and disappear. I knew because it happened so often but I also recognized that I had no control over when the next show would begin or end. It was a good lesson in enjoying the moment without exerting my will on the event.

A raft load of kelp floated by. I thought about how clocks had become unnecessary, calendars and efficiency irrelevant. Control belonged to the weather and to the ocean.

Every day was a blank, blue, twenty-four-hour sheet of time. Our only calendar was the sticky kind you get at the dry cleaners. I could draw a circle or an "X" over a date but there wasn't room to write anything. Before we went cruising, I stuck the calendar to the inside of the galley cupboard as a joke. As a family, we had held periodic calendar meetings to catch up on each other's schedules. Life without a day-planner was like hitting bottom on a long bungee cord. When the bouncing stopped and after a long deep inhale, I discovered that it was liberating to not be needed somewhere on a daily basis.

The ocean is an unpredictable place to live, which made planning and punctuality not only impossible but irrelevant. I'd been raised on a steady diet of efficiency and these were difficult lessons for me.

Boaters say that a cruiser with a plane to meet is an unsafe sailor. Adding a deadline to the cruising life encourages us to ignore the weather conditions. Being controlled by the calendar or the clock is foolhardy. Putting the concept of time on the back burner was a wonderful release that allowed me a sense of freedom I hadn't known before.

Part of the control I'd had over my life was that I was seldom in a position where I could get lost. Yet I yearned to be a little lost. In the sixth grade, my friend, Sue and I rode our bicycles after school in search of roads we hadn't ridden before, seeking the allure of the unknown. When we were in our 20s, Sue followed the road to adventure, first as an airline stewardess, then traveling the world and learning languages. I didn't. I had gotten married and made babies. When the girls were toddlers, I'd strap them into their seats and drive around my home town, trying to get lost. Occasionally, I got a little turned around but never thoroughly lost. I was married to the wrong man, living the Junior League lifestyle and stuck geographically less than five miles from where I'd been born. My life was off course, but I couldn't seem to get physically lost. Now, sailing the west coast of Mexico, I was married to the right man, free to do as I wished and confused about my geography most of the time. It felt good.

We ate when we were hungry and wore clothes when we wanted to. I chose to be topless depending on the weather and my mood. It wasn't a sexy preference, I went naked to keep my clothes clean and dry. I also liked the way the breezes caressed my skin and I became a more sensual woman, less concerned about rules and protocol.

Our world stretched to the horizon and the sameness seemed to go on forever. So did the relentless sun. Sailing into infinity looks idyllic but we had very little shade and no relief from the intense heat. Our canvas dodger was small and shaded only a few feet of the cockpit. My skin responded with heat rashes and blisters. Just when I thought I couldn't take it any longer, something wonderful would appear: dolphin dances, shimmering stars, the legendary green flash at sunset. We swam with sea turtles and dolphins and I gave a ride to an octopus that attached itself to my swim fin.

Nature's surprises were the good news that I clung to during difficult times. One evening, Rick dumped the dishwater out of the rinse bucket and a dinner plate along with it. I wanted him to pay more attention to details. He told me to "lighten up." But I'm organized while Rick is more relaxed. He likes to quietly solve problems after they happen. I want to talk about it and take preventive steps.

"What's the big deal? We'll buy another damn plate."

"That's not the point. You should have been more careful."

"Do you want me to swim after it?"

"Of course not. I want you to apologize."

"I said I'm sorry it happened."

"I want you to be sorry you did it."

"I'm sorry, too. Sorry you're being such a bitch."

In the confines of a small boat our differences ballooned and popped. The little explosions were like bubbles bursting but later we couldn't remember what we'd argued about.

THE OCEAN IS ...

capricious   repetitious
moody   fierce
full of life   powerful
sparkling   enchanting
exhausting   inspiring
raging   placid
ever changing   unpredictable
and so am I.

> "Once upon a time, there was a woman who discovered she had turned into the wrong person. Give her credit: most people her age would say it was too late to make any change. What's done is done, they would say. No use trying to alter things at this late date.
> It did occur to her to say that. But she didn't."
>
> ANNE TYLER,
> BACK WHEN WE WERE GROWNUPS, 2001

CHAPTER 9

Baggage

RICK WAS DOING his morning calisthenics on the bow while I huddled in the corner of the cockpit reading recipes in *The Cruising Chef*. We needed the thirty feet between us. Most of the time, Rick and I were perfect partners but proximity was putting pressure on our personality differences. Underway we seldom fought, I reflected. It was at anchor or in a marina that we were more likely to froth and foam.

We'd been anchored in the bay for a week. During breakfast Rick had been pensive. "What's on your mind? You're awfully quiet," I said.

"I'm thinking that we need talk about this circumnavigation idea. It's too big," he answered.

"What?" I was appalled. Pissed. "No way. You're nuts. Damn you," I'd hollered at him, throwing a slice of toast on my plate so hard that it bounced.

"Well, you asked me what I was thinking and that's your answer."

We were both intimidated by the size of the ocean between here and wherever we were going but we hadn't said it out loud before.

Rick seemed to be heaving the weights with more aggression than usual. Our little black-and-white cow still swung from her post on the railing, but she looked a little weather worn. Her gentle swaying was hypnotic.

Alice in Wonderland's King of Hearts had said to the White Rabbit, "Begin at the beginning and keep going till you come to the end. Then stop." I liked the logic but where was our ending, the place we should stop? I abandoned menu planning and picked up my journal. My emotions arced and swayed like nimble tree branches in a gale.

> There's someone hiding inside. I hear her pounding on my skull, demanding her turn. I wonder if it's the child I used to be, the one I might have been, or maybe the adult I'm becoming. I think about those who successfully let their twin selves act out. The accountant who became a watercolor artist. The engineer who crafts a suspense novel. But why don't they become full-time painters or writers? We forgo our very nature, like living the life of a hippo when I'm really a bird.
>
> Cosmetic surgery would change how I look but not how I see. A business card doesn't change who

> I am. My psychic baggage is packed with my boat gear just as efficiently as it controlled my land life. But now I have the time to embrace my creativity, my individuality. The thought of turning my back on all this freedom makes me shudder. Going back would extinguish the fire I'm fanning. I'm afraid to propel forward but more fearful of going back.

I tried to make sense of my confusion.

I spent my childhood at one address but Rick attended fourteen schools before high school. After college he kept drifting, always drifting, searching for contentment by moving from Massachusetts to Hawaii to California to Oregon. He was searching for something he couldn't define, surrounding himself with a surrogate family of co-workers and athletes, car salesmen and racquetball partners. And he thought he was happy. It was only in retrospect that he voiced a realization of how shallow that happiness had been. His "family" had been a troupe of malcontents searching for roots, for constancy, for purpose in their lives.

When Rick met the girls and me, we became his family and he became "Dad." He was lavish with hugs and humor and consistent with limits and support for the girls' dreams. I looked at his tan legs pumping up and down in repetitive lifts. His hairy chest was bronze and he was growing a new beard. How could I be so furious with him?

Rick is one of those rare people who doesn't measure people by their appearance but by their behavior. He's judicious and honest. I'd seen him be equally generous with kind words at a fast food drive-up window as he was to employees and bosses.

Raised in an Air Force family, he'd spent significant time in forty-six of the fifty states but I wasn't so adept at changing geography. And my failed first marriage left a scar on my ability to blindly follow. I prodded the cow, making her flip so high she swung around the stainless railing. "Okay, if cows can fly, maybe I can too," I mumbled.

My Dad was raised in poverty and joined the Army right after high school. He married Mom at the end of the war and entered the business world. They rode the crest of the post–World War II boom so I was born into a world bulging with possibility.

Five mornings a week Dad put on a fresh-from-the-cleaners starched white shirt, smart cuff links at the wrists and a tie knotted firmly at his throat. He read the morning paper while Mom cooked his bacon and egg breakfast. At precisely 7:45 AM he drove his new-every-three-years white Chrysler into the city to make enough money so it never needed to be discussed. Mom did volunteer work and had dinner and a scotch waiting when he returned punctually at 6:00 PM. For forty years.

While they marched to a disciplined drummer, Mom and Dad dished out lots of love. Mom read to us from a carefully selected stock of fairy tales with happy endings. She drove us to piano lessons and swimming pools, telling my brother, sister and me with every hug and kiss that we were the most wonderful children on earth, full of possibility beyond all imagining. I was the middle kid, sandwiched comfortably between an older brother and a younger sister. I basked in the comfort zone of being neither first nor last.

We lived on an acre at the top of a hill. Being a "hill person," as my classmates described those of us who had views instead of sidewalks, was all I ever knew. When I first crawled to a window to pull myself up, the view from the floor to ceiling windows looked down on the pointy tops of fir trees that poked the clouds above the city of Portland. My brother and I learned our numbers counting bridges over the Willamette River.

With all that opportunity at my feet, reasonable people might conclude that a young girl would dream high-minded dreams and have powerful career goals. But they would be wrong. To my young eyes, it seemed as though all a person had to do was show up and a transcript for a successful life would roll out of the typewriter.

I had a vague notion that I was lucky but I wanted sidewalks and kids next door to play with. In high school, I longed to be in the popular group and I hovered around the edges of the cool cliques. I joined the debate and golf teams. I was on the dance team, I had boyfriends and when I didn't I still had dates. I got good grades but I had no vision of what to do with my life other than to choose which skirt and sweater to wear.

The 1960s were the Age of Aquarius and Woodstock. We had a powerboat named *Aquarius* but that had more to do with the symbolism of water than the Age. I did well in school because it was expected, not because of inspiration or career plans. Growing up in the Land of Oz, I emerged as a capable and inquisitive young woman, but I was naïve, presuming that life would be smooth sailing without much initiative on my part.

A high school counselor suggested I apply to an Ivy League school, or at least to some college on the East Coast. Dad said, "You can go to school anywhere you want as long as it's in Eugene, Oregon." Humor wasn't in his repertoire, even though he smiled as he said it. It was a Father Knows Best world and I was a good kid. I enrolled at the University of Oregon.

When the posh sororities dropped me from their rush lists, I sobbed the tears of a heartbroken seventeen-year-old. I wanted to belong and I was as certain as any teenager that no one who mattered would ever want me. I carried the adolescent need for conformity into my forties and onto the sailboat.

The tether that was our family's anchor held me firmly in place. I wasn't offered release from the bonds, but I didn't think to ask, either. When I should have been finding who "me" was, I wasn't. I had no clue what to do with my life. Self-confidence ran through my veins but all I knew for sure was to look my best, to say nice things and to be on time. I guess that's why we were Presbyterians and golfers: well-dressed and punctual.

I got a degree in English for lack of a better idea and married the man I was dating when I graduated. Continuing my legacy of conformity, I became my mother. The movie *Runaway Bride* gave a funny twist to the dilemma when Julia Roberts' character ordered her eggs cooked the way her current boyfriend liked his. She was a chameleon, adapting and changing rather than finding her own path. As a mother, I did that, too. Just like my mother, I ate burned toast because no one else would. We said we liked it but I had no idea what I liked.

I nibbled my meals from toddler scraps while my husband strayed. The divorce after a decade was inevitable but was followed quickly by meeting and marrying Rick. Another decade passed, punctuated by errands, appointments, work schedules and brief vacations. Then the girls went to college and I was effectively fired from full-time parenting.

I pulled my journal onto my lap.

> Sometimes I'm miserable on this tiny boat in a huge ocean but more often I love it. Happiness surges into view like a dolphin but retreats, reappearing on the horizon at odd intervals, dancing around me.
>
> I can't sail without Rick and I wouldn't want to go anywhere without him anyway. If a lap around the world is too big, too scary, we'll scale the plan to something smaller. Maybe the Panama Canal

> and the Caribbean. OK - a left at the bottom of Mexico instead of a right across the ocean.

I laid my journal on top of the yellow cookbook.
"Hey sweetie," I called to Rick. "How 'bout the Caribbean next year?"

> *"There are only two ways to live your life.
> One is as though nothing is a miracle.
> The other is as though everything is."*
>
> ALBERT EINSTEIN

CHAPTER 10

Alive

WE SAT TOGETHER in the cockpit when rain suddenly peppered the sea. Each drop pierced the surface like the needle of a sewing machine at full speed. Sheets of water collided with the ocean and bounced, causing mayhem on water that just moments earlier had been still.

Instinctively, we jumped off the cushions and leapt under the canvas dodger.

"Oh my gosh. It's raining," I said, stripping out of my clothes and tossing them into the cabin. We'd been sailing in Mexico for more than a year and this was just our third rain shower.

"Nice suit," Rick said while he, too, undressed.

I stepped into the rain, arms raised to the heavens, and Rick followed me. Within minutes we were dancing in a rendition of the tribal dance from the movie *Wind*. It can't have been pretty but there was no one to watch.

Rain bounced off *Nanook*'s deck, her sails and railings. Rick connected a funnel that led to a bucket, saving some of the precious fresh water.

While the boat was getting a bath, we scrubbed ourselves and then each other. Just as we finished rinsing our bodies in the flood, the rain stopped. The decks were clean and so were we. The air was warm and the smell of freshly scrubbed wet skin was sexy. The sea was calm. We lay down on the cockpit cushions and enjoyed each other.

Rick went below to check our course. Lying on a sail bag, I watched the clouds play charades. A breeze rearranged them. A pirate? A banana. Light globes. Italy. So many shapes.

Rick called out that our *Charlie's Charts* cruising guide noted submerged volcanic rocks on this southerly approach to our anchorage. I abandoned my game and stood at the bow rail, on watch for hull crunchers. The ocean was dark turquoise, thirty feet deep and clear.

If I'd been sitting down we might have run over the turtle instead of changing course. The first one arched his neck and looked at me with eyes that seemed to hold ancient wisdom. I stared, pointed and shouted, "Wow!"

"What is it?" Rick called.

If I was supposed to be on watch, I would need to be more specific. "It's a turtle," I shouted over my shoulder.

"Port or starboard?"

"Both, everywhere." The surface was littered with what looked like trash can lids, the forty-gallon yard debris kind. Rick stood on the cockpit bench, steering *Nanook* around the turtles. We zigzagged like a drunk to avoid hitting them. They were scattered at random over a half mile of flat seas.

Leaving the turtles, we approached *Isla Isabela*. The 150-foot towering rocks that distinguish the island welcomed us. The towers are called *Los Manos*, the hands. They reach skyward in a prayerful pose and we dropped anchor in their shadow in twenty-five feet of water.

We lunched on chorizo and tomato quesadillas in the cockpit and watched the water dance. Isla Isabela is a marine sanctuary and fish flipped and flopped out of the sea.

Dolphins raced around the hull. A manta ray performed gymnastics and landed with a splat. His two-foot wingspan sent up a dramatic spray. One after another, rays took flight and landed like kites crashing in the sand.

We hadn't finished lunch when a furious splashing about one hundred yards off the stern caught our attention. I grabbed the binoculars and saw a whale thrashing with an intensity indicating extreme distress. Her glistening back shone like a boulder in the bright sunshine but she shook like a 7.5 earthquake was rocking her.

Handing the binoculars to Rick, I said, "What do you think's wrong?"

He watched the gyrating whale and said, "It looks like she's trying to shake something from her tail."

It could have been a fishing line, a plastic bag or a

piece of trash that was caught on her tail. We handed the binoculars back and forth, abandoned our lunch plates and spoke in hushed tones.

I sat in the corner of the cockpit, arms wrapped around my knees, squinting over the railing. Rick stood next to me with his hands on my shoulders. We watched in despair at the picture unfolding in front of us. It looked as though trash must be the culprit and we felt somehow responsible just because the problem looked man-made.

As the minutes crept by, our attention turned to the whale's timing. She took breaks from her gyrations at regular intervals. Two minutes of furious splashing was followed by thirty seconds of quiet. And it repeated. Again. And again. Even with the aid of high-powered binoculars, we couldn't identify the reason.

It went on for nearly an hour before the thrashing stopped. It was Rick who figured out what we might be witnessing. "Holy mother of ...," Rick began, handing me the binoculars.

"What is it?" I said, reaching for them and raising them to my eyes in a single motion.

Off the stern of our boat, clearly in view, we watched the baby whale's arrival. First the tail. Then the head. Within just a few minutes, mom and calf slipped away. The water rippled and calmed. With tears running down our cheeks, we sat in reverent silence.

Later I asked a naturalist at a presentation on whales what kind it might have been. He said that it was most likely a blue whale and that what we had witnessed was very rare. Our research revealed that blue whales are huge, long and slender, with shades of bluish-gray and somewhat lighter underneath. That didn't match what we had seen and Rick and I concluded it was more likely a pilot whale, which is jet black or dark gray. The description of the pilot whale's smaller, elongated but stocky-in-the-tail-fin shape, was what we saw. The birth weight would have been about 100 pounds. Whatever type it was, I was grateful we had been there, quietly watching a whale being born.

Isla Isabela is a good overnight stop between *Mazatlan* and *Puerto Vallarta* but we stayed much longer. In the daytime, the island is populated by researchers and the sailors who anchor in the bay. At night, the people retreat and thousands of birds have the place to themselves.

Isabela would be paradise if you lost your sense of smell. I got a lesson in the nastiness of the pervasive poop and my shorts were testimony to the power of green goo. I fell once getting out of the dinghy and twice on the rocks. From the waist down I was slathered and spattered with bird dung. Rick's only visible sign of the slime was a half-dozen smudges on his socks and calves.

Across the island, frigates, gulls, terns, boobies and cormorants staked claim to their own area and didn't cross over. Green-footed boobies clustered on the pebbled shore next to the red-footed neighborhood, the blue-footed congregated nearby, but never trespassing. Frigates had their own piece of real estate while the terns took the low ground and the cormorants commanded the hillsides.

Apparently, fertility wasn't a problem because bird eggs were everywhere. Every tuft of grass, 'Y'-shaped branch and cluster of rocks held a nest. It looked as though a tennis ball machine had gone berserk. Eggs larger than Rick's fist were on every hillock and ledge. We had to duck, bend and step carefully to avoid disturbing them. It was a danger-strewn walk through the egg factory.

Boobies are large birds with tapered wings and long bills. The most common was the blue-footed. I waltzed in front of them, imitating their movement. My rubber-soled shoes were light blue and I felt like one of the gang. It wouldn't have surprised me if they'd burst into a chorus of Elvis Presley's "get offa my blue suede shoes" and I hummed a few bars to encourage them.

The boobies dove from the rocks for their dinner, chasing their prey underwater. Like teenagers, they left their belongings everywhere. Booby eggs were scattered on the ground and in nests on low bushes.

The other species that captured our imaginations was the frigate. Sometimes called pirate birds, they look like the pelican but with the aura of a prehistoric pterodactyl with an arched wing plane and long narrow tails.

Frigates are massive with iridescent black feathers and a five-foot wingspan. Their primal mating ritual is a spectacle. The male puffs his chest, looking as if he swallowed an inflated red balloon. The frigates soar in circles over the ocean and pluck their prey with barely a ripple in the sea.

The problem in the frigate neighborhood, too, was that as we ducked under branches we couldn't help but come close to the nests and eggs. We moved carefully around low-hanging branches to avoid bumping a nest or causing the frigate so much grief that he'd upset the nest himself. Frigates don't swim, can't walk well and can't take off from a flat surface. They're aerial and the sky was thick with the circling, cawing, black birds. If the movie *The Birds* scared you, do not go to *Isla Isabela*.

From the hilltop, the water was wavy turquoise and we could see marine life even from this height. A pod of pilot whales cruised by. They swam in a large circle and dove like slow-motion dolphins.

We walked along the cliff and stopped when hundreds of red and black crabs clattered over the rocks and scuttled away. It was rush hour on crab highway.

Making our way around the back of the island we saw that it was birthing season for the pelicans as well. Featherless babies squawked in their nests and eggs that were ready to crack rocked in the crooks of branches.

The next day, from the cockpit of *Nanook*, we saw the pelicans in action. Thousands of the brown warriors arrived from the west, in a re-enactment of the assault on Pearl Harbor. They came in low, hovering in precision formation before they split the water like bombs in a series of massive explosions. I wondered how they kept from colliding.

Mid-morning, we were surrounded by puffer fish. I netted one. The little guy looked as if he'd been designed by Walt Disney. In my green fish net, he puffed, puckered, let out a little cry and burped a big bubble of water. I laughed at his cartoon antics and gently put him back. In a very short time they disappeared.

It was hot so we put on our scuba gear and spent the afternoon underwater. We wore diving gloves and Rick carried a collection sack at his waist. I called it a grocery bag. For the next two hours we floated in a Jacques Cousteau world.

Turtles swam above us and neon blue and yellow Sergeant Majors swirled in front of my mask. A cone shaped scallop snapped shut when I touched it and Rick used his knife to pry it loose from the rock it had hinged itself to. He dropped the eight-inch shell into his mesh loot bag. He took my hand and we hovered twenty feet below the surface. The motion of the water tugged at us and turned us into ocean puppets. Tall strands of sea grass swayed to music I couldn't hear and triggerfish peeked through. It was a hypnotic ballet and I had a season's pass.

Rick pointed at something to his left and I turned to see what had gotten his attention. It was a pumpkin-orange lobster decorated with cobalt blue dots. With four strong breaststroke pulls, Rick plucked the lobster from the ocean floor before it could scoot into its rock cave. The lobster joined three scallops and a dozen choc-

olate clams in the bag. The meal prep side of my brain was making elaborate plans.

Back onboard, the setting sun dried our skin. We were treated to another rainbow sunset, my favorite kind. The sky draped a turquoise, pink and purple sash above the water and reflected it back on the ocean in shades of red, yellow and orange.

At the sound of an outboard motor approaching, I put down my wine glass and stood up, waving. The *panga* driver silenced the motor and held onto our railing with his left hand. In his right hand was a bucket that he handed to Rick for inspection. Five small *huachinango*. We happily paid him fourteen *pesos* for the fresh red snapper fillets.

While we waited for the water to boil to cook the lobster, a half dozen dolphins arrived. They took turns breaking the surface, dancing and whistling. They were the kind we saw most often and we called them "common dolphins." One turned on its side and slapped its fin, sending a spray into the cockpit. I laughed. Wiping the sea water from my face, I said, "There's nothing common about a dolphin show."

Later, I basted the red snapper inside and out with lime juice, mayonnaise and pepper. Baked in the oven for twenty minutes, they were *muy sabroso*.

Sailboats in all shapes and sizes came and went in the small anchorage, but we stayed. With his snorkel mask and fins on, Rick spent hours examining the sail drive on our engine. He cleaned the vents and that helped the overheating problem. An engineer in the anchorage switched a plug on our alternator to boost our recharge capabilities. It was all a work in progress.

> *"If change is the essence of existence, one would have thought it only sensible to make it the premise of our philosophy."*
>
> SOMERSET MAUGHAM,
> *THE RAZOR'S EDGE*

CHAPTER 11

Bahía Banderas

THE FIRST HINT that we might be lured to sea was the briefest of encounters off the *malecon* (boardwalk) at *Puerto Vallarta*. Rick had won a sales bonus trip soon after we were married. At the end of our week in the sun, we were gazing out to sea when an aged sailboat passed by. The skipper wore a floppy canvas hat and little else. We waved and he waved back.

Rick had looked at me and said, "What's wrong with that picture?"

I don't remember what I said but the southbound sailor wasn't going back to work and we were. He looked like he didn't have a care in the world and the image stayed with us.

Now, approaching the PV marina, Rick dropped the sails and I held the tiller. Until recently, I had avoided steering in close quarters. A heavy sailboat maintains its momentum and I had no feel for how fast or slow I should be going as we approached a pier. I'd tried it a few times, but I'd scraped the side of the dock or narrowly missed running into another boat, incidents that scattered my confidence like rose petals in a gale. I relegated myself to deckhand duties where I couldn't do any damage. Until Rick played a trick on me.

When we needed to change slips in *Mazatlan*, Rick had stood on the dock guiding *Nanook* out but when he should have stepped onboard, he gave the bow a little shove instead. With a grin and a wave, he said, "You can do it, honey, I'll catch the line at B14." I had no choice but to stay at the helm and remember to breathe.

Being in a marina was a trade-off. Our world went from less than one hundred square feet and just the two of us to a community of boaters, restaurants and shopping. Since we didn't use the dinghy we had dry fannies and wore shoes, too. Most marinas had tiled bathrooms for a proper shower and some even had air-conditioned television rooms. It was really very civilized.

Now in *Puerto Vallarta*, we headed to town to do the procedural check-in with the authorities. Back and forth we went between the offices of the Port Captain, Immigration and Customs. Why weren't they in the same building and open the same hours?

I was hot and tired, but over a beer and a terra-cotta bowl of comfort food, spicy *queso fundido* and corn tortillas, I remembered that it had been hard to understand behaviors in our previous lives, too. Why were seat belts required in cars but not on buses? Why did we vote near home on a weekday when people were miles away at work? If I couldn't explain my own culture, I counseled, it was hopeless to think I could comprehend foreign logic. I scraped the last of the warm cheese from the bowl with a broken chip and told Rick what one of my Spanish teachers had told me.

Felipe had said that to understand Mexico would be like peeling the thin layers from a pearl. Each layer would reveal a different level of understanding. I liked the image of Mexico as a pearl, revealing itself one thin layer at a time. If that was true, I said, "then America must be an onion, much easier to peel with just a few thick layers." Rick looked at me like I had gone a little nuts.

After lunch we caught a bus that we hoped would take us to the working side of town. *Nanook* needed new batteries. With recent replacements, one bank was now a Mexican brand and the second set were American gel cells. We'd been told that consistency might help our charging problems.

Cruisers are always in search of parts for repair jobs. It's similar to the scope of repairs you'd need if a twenty-five-year-old house was rocked side to side and parked in warm salt water. Add a scavenger hunt to find the parts to the necessity of doing the repairs yourself and you've pretty much grasped the reality of cruising.

Back at the boat, we hauled the anchor chain onto

the dock and checked every link, removing loose ones and painting the anchor windlass. Rick pulled out the new bilge pump he'd put in backward and reinstalled it. We laid the head hoses out on the dock and pounded the sludge out of them, sanded and revarnished the rails and repaired our torn bug screens.

On day three in the engine room, Rick had gone from confused interest and curiosity, through frustration, into total involvement. "There's water in the oil. Could be from following seas." He sounded unconvinced. He changed the oil twice to flush the system. It was hot in the engine room and demoralizing to be working so hard and accomplishing *nada*.

We also had cavitation that started at 1800 rpm. The vibrations shook the floorboards like a washing machine gyrating an uneven load. A prop engineer at a local machine shop modified it, confident it would give us the needed rpm, but it didn't.

Rick's a big guy so folding himself like a paperclip into small spaces was not something he did well. Most of the men in the cruising fleet were tinkerers. They seemed to enjoy puttering around their boats looking for things to fix but Rick's a guy who's used to results, not repetition. Feeling unsuccessful caused menopausal behavior, not a pretty sight in a man. Besides, I thought menopausal mood swings were my personal perogative. When Rick and I were both overheated and verbal about it, the result was volatile.

I wrote in my journal:

> The engine is no longer intermittently difficult; it's a constant problem. Cruising isn't much fun when we've stuck in a marina and always repairing something. I just wish Rick would focus on what I think is important.

Uh-oh. I put down my pen and looked at what I'd written. Did I really believe that if I could magically alter him to my complete satisfaction I'd like the result? If I had just one wave of a magic wand wouldn't it cause a domino effect and change the things I love, too? Probably, I mused.

Mosquitos buzzed my ears and were making me cranky. "He's imperfect and he's mine," I thought, swatting a mosquito on my cheek. "And I love him. I'm also furious with him for being different from me and so damn close by. I wish I could just go somewhere and give us some space from each other. But I couldn't get in a car or go to a mall for some recreational shopping. I threw down my journal and looked out to sea. A powerful longing to be a dolphin came over me.

One day, I met a gal on the dock. Her name was Pat Henry. She was a celebrity of sorts because she was in her sixties and had just completed a single-handed circumnavigation on her thirty-one–foot sailboat, *Southern Cross*. I couldn't imagine that much aloneness, thousands of miles of ocean with no one to share it. Pat is the oldest North American woman to solo circumnavigate and we became friends, sharing our writing at a PV critique group while she was crafting her story, published by McGraw-Hill under the title *By the Grace of the Sea*. I asked Pat, "Does a sunrise look as sweet when you see it alone?"

"Christie, when I'm with someone, I wonder what they're thinking and if they're enjoying it. And then we need to talk."

"And you'd rather not?" We were obviously so different. I couldn't imagine spending even a week alone but she had sailed the world's oceans without someone to hug, to depend on, to love, for eight long years. It was a reminder of how many ways there are to shape a life.

Sailing taught me first hand that all I really needed to be content was something to eat and somewhere to sleep. And someone special to do it with. I decided to count my blessings instead of troubles.

To our cruising friends we were Rick and Christie, the *Nanookers*. None of us used last names; they were irrelevant. Neither did we know what kinds of careers our boating friends had left. Conversations tacked between ports of call and favorite lobster dives. With oceans of free time, we dove into topics such as how to cook triggerfish and octopus and where to buy sewing needles or a new bath towel.

We met Ray and Lucy on *Pepina Rae*, from Louisiana. They told stories of dripping moss, cheap housing and humidity. The way they described it, a boat could grow moss on its headliners in just two weeks. I longed to see New Orleans and to experience Creole cooking. I wanted to be there, heck, I wanted to be everywhere, but would we get there on *Nanook*? I didn't know anymore.

Boats came and went and that was one of the delights of cruising. New compadres. We joked that we could close escrow in thirty minutes by simply stowing the dock lines or pulling up the anchor.

As in the suburbs, marina life included a balance of routine. Breakfast was coffee and cereal or yogurt with fruit. Rick would tackle a boat project or work out in the marina-resort's gym. I did a boat project or wrote, scribbling on a legal pad or banging on the old typewriter I had on board.

We played cards or games. We took the bus into town to visit the dentist, to get a haircut, and to locate parts. We took a bus to the golf course. We held a book swap in our cockpit and sold T-shirts for a local regatta. The week before Christmas the cruising fleet magically came up with strings of lights to run up their masts and wreaths to festoon on their boats.

I took over the chairmanship of a project to help a local orphange, *Casa Hogar*. Lots of the ladies had sewing machines for repairing sails, upholstering cushions, and whatever else people with that talent do. I think I failed Home Ec but I could organize and motivate so I assembled a crew of sailors to improve conditions at the orphange. Twelve women made curtains from donated fabric. Twenty men painted the exterior of the building. Four of us rounded up chests of drawers and clothing racks and found cars to deliver them. My life was returning to suburban routines.

I learned to play tennis. Marina guests enjoyed the same benefits as hotel guests and that included tennis, according to skill levels. I joined the beginners and Rick was so advanced that when the resident pro took a vacation during our stay, the hotel hired Rick to be the replacement.

The resort folks we met on the tennis courts and around the pool would probably have been shocked to know that we could live for two to three months on their one-week hotel bill. A week or ten days was all most of these vacationers would get but this was my life. I reflected that it would be easy to fall into the trap of taking it for granted and seeing the boat breakdowns as insurmountable problems. "Perspective...it's all about perspective," I thought.

I enrolled in a Spanish class that met three days a week. I liked being a student and the aspect of needing to be somewhere at a specific time. It felt familiar. There were a dozen of us with varying levels of expertise. I had advanced to learning about direct and indirect objects, two versions of each tense: present, future and past. I practiced my Spanish everywhere I went.

A message from Downwind Marine in San Diego came to us on the Single Side Band radio. They had sent a package on a boat, we had no idea which one, to *Zihuatanejo*. We had ordered a few items and hoped the package en route was a new prop and six oil filters. We hadn't thought to ask the very important details of who, what and when. Those were questions that would have been first on our minds when we were part of the efficient world to our north. Here, we were simply happy that a parcel with our name on it was southbound.

Some cruisers get so comfortable in a marina that they never leave. We didn't plan to be permanent, but we did settle into a land life. Birds swooped low in fluid contrast to the hundreds of masts that stood unnaturally still. Rick and I kept our eyes on those birds, wanting to soar freely again and not to get sucked into the vortex of being permanent marina rats.

Leaving *Puerto Vallarta*, it was a short, brisk downwind sail to the anchorage in front of the village of *La Crux de Huanacaxtle*. We made it even faster by flying the spinnaker in addition to the main. Our first attempt to put up the spinnaker had been a disaster. We'd deployed the chute wrong and sailed over it, turning it into a sling under our keel instead of a billowing kite off the bow. But now the green and yellow nylon stripes were flying proudly, ballooning in the wind and covering the miles quickly.

Nanook had been a good coach. Her rigging hollered when I was neglectful or distracted and she hummed with happiness when I got it right. All I had to do was listen and I had learned how to sail.

We rode the dinghy through the surf, cut the outboard and hopped out. It was evening and insects made halos around the street lamps and neighbors chatted in doorways. Older folks sitting on plastic chairs swirled the humid air with paper fans. Through an open door, a framed picture of the Virgin Mary was illuminated by a candle on a plastic tablecloth. Children played in the hard-packed dirt, drawing circles with sticks in the red dust and chasing each other in an informal game of tag, demonstrating that laughter makes the same sound in all languages.

With its enormous view of the sea, the cobbled patio at *Dos Felipes* was popular with boaters. Tables rocked on the uneven ground and full mugs of tepid beer sloshed. This Tuesday night, the patio buzzed with the voices of cruisers whose homes were floating at anchor in the bay. Under a sky crowded with stars, guitarists strolled among the tables, collecting a few pesos for every song.

A young girl came to our table to see if we wanted another beer. She wore second-skin jeans and a white blouse, ruffled at the scooped neck and bare at the midriff. Her arms were bronze and smooth, her feet bare, her eyes sparkling chestnut. The gleaming smile caught my attention like a firefly.

"*Quisiera dos más cervezas?*" she asked.

"*Si, por favor,*" we replied in unison.

We listened to the newer arrivals tell stories of sailing south to Mexico. Some recounted tales of storms, torn sails, or a dinghy lost in a rough passage. One was a harrowing story by a couple who had tried to enter an anchorage in the dark and had narrowly escaped losing their boat on the rocks. But most were simple stories, like ours, of sailing with dolphins and taking pleasure in the star-filled skies, vibrant sunrises and sunsets. A friend asked Rick to share the story of our close encounter with a freighter. And he did.

"One morning we were having breakfast, seated on opposite sides of the cockpit. The air was dead calm, the ocean flat as a table. Christie had turned the radio off to silence the whistling fishermen and their codes. It was barely 9:00 AM and hot. And just like that," Rick said snapping his fingers, "it got dark. I shot to my feet and Christie did what women do, she screamed."

Amused chuckles came from our pals at the tables.

Rick continued. "There was a freighter about two hundred yards off our port and closing in. He cast a long shadow. It was like a skyscraper sliding toward us. Green, white, red and blue containers were stacked like Legos into the air, blocking the sun. I fired up the engine and yanked the tiller.

"It turned out that the crew was bored and wanted to see who we were and couldn't raise us on the radio. Scared the shit out of us, though. Christie flipped our radio on and talked to them. It was a small German container ship, but it didn't look small to us. They thanked us for our time and motored off. They disappeared over the horizon in less than fifteen minutes. Now we have a rule. One of us is on watch even in the daytime."

Stories flowed. We ate *hamburguesas con queso* and sipped our Coronas. Herb and Marsha on *Wispern* said they were going to focus on land travel, returning to the boat between trips. In the spring they would truck

Wispern to San Francisco, buy a condo and sail there. Cruisers were always changing their plans.

Stories from boats that had summered in the Sea of Cortez unfolded. *Tortuga* had been hit by lightning and *Moonshadow* was knocked down by a water spout. Miseries included heat-blistered skin, moldy headliners, green fur growing in water hoses, and violent wind, but they had formed close friendships, lazed in the sunshine and snorkeled for food.

In the months before we left our jobs, men spoke eagerly of following us, leaving work and the suburbs for a few months, at least. Women were far more skeptical. How could I live without a large closet and a refrigerator? Did I really want to spend 24/7 with my husband and no car to get away in order to pursue my own passions? I tried to explain, but their skepticism remained. I had wanted these women to understand me. I craved a sisterhood of soul mates that I never found in the sorority, the PTA, in coworkers or with neighbors. I didn't find it until we were cruising and then it was everywhere.

Living the life of a nomad, I was with kindred spirits, a family of sorts. We were bound not by similar profession or zip code but by a shared passion.

My sense of place found roots when the fragrance of a fruit stand mingled with salt air. My pulse quickened when the drum beat of the pounding surf layered itself on the song of morning roosters. These sensory moments were sweetened by the cadence of the Spanish language. It happened, too, in magical places where we stayed long enough that the vegetable cart lady knew my name and handed me the perfect tomato hidden in the back of her truck. And when the shrimper bagged eight shelled beauties before I said a word.

Draining our beers and yawning, we strolled toward the beach to head home. We dragged our dinghy on wheels into the sea until I was hip deep in water. I scrambled over the side, Rick gave a final push, jumped in and yanked the outboard's starter cord. Slightly off shore and out of the surf, he idled the motor, released the cotter pins and lifted the wheels. It was as automatic as buckling a seat belt had been in our land lives.

Onboard, we attached the dinghy's sling, cranked her out of the water and fell into a comfortable sleep in the womb of the V-berth.

I was awake at dawn, roused by roosters, barking dogs and Pedro's bell ringing. I turned the propane on under the percolator and climbed into the cockpit. A violet light cracked the horizon and the ocean had the look of a wrinkled green sheet. Squinting into the sunlight, I counted at least thirty sailboats in the anchorage.

The smell of wood smoke hung in the morning air. A new arrival circled, looking for a place to drop the anchor. I waved at the woman on the bow and she waved back. We weren't the only ones who had quit our jobs, sold the cars and left to go sailing. We met hundreds of fellow cruisers, long-time married couples in their 50s and 60s, sailing for an open-ended period of time. Most were experienced sailors and many of the men were engine room geeks, which Rick wasn't.

Rick also didn't search the boat for maintenance projects. After every sail, our clothes had been wet, then wetter for the last few months. Obviously, the ocean was leaking into the bow lockers under our mattresses. Rick had inspected with a flashlight and examined the caulking under the bow railing. Nothing looked wrong and we weren't sinking so he postponed any solutions. Salt water leaves a sticky residue so we did the laundry more often.

I pulled a damp shirt from the locker and pulled it over my head. "Stinks like socks," I grumbled.

Living on a boat I was more dependent on Rick than I'd been in a house. In the suburbs, I could drive to the store but at sea I couldn't lift the dinghy or hoist the anchor without Rick. I could hang a picture on sheetrock but on a boat you can't just pound a nail when you feel like it.

To appease my nagging, Rick stood in the dinghy and smeared new caulking goo under the cap rail.

"If you'd done that in the marina it would have been easier," I said to Rick from the bow.

"If, if, if," I thought he muttered. He'd known me long enough to try silence as a way to shut me up. The dinghy bounced under his feet and the mud brown caulk line smeared on the cream-colored fiberglass hull.

I hated wet clothes and hated the mess Rick had made stabbing at the repair job.

We went ashore for lunch while the mess dried. Sitting on stools on the second floor of at our favorite taco bar, we kept our volume down if not our tempers. Two iguanas cavorted on the adjoining rooftop, taunting each other.

"Hey, look at those guys," Rick said. "They look as pissed off as we are."

They entertained us and we didn't have to talk to each other.

The iguanas were more than two feet long and glowed like emeralds on the shiny tin roof. They chased and teased until one gave a come-hither lift of the chin and their heads reared back in unison. The playmate scurried over. The way she greeted him I realized they had been dancing to court, to mate, and to seal their bond.

My hand snaked across the table and caught Rick's. We smiled at each other and returned our attention to the iguana show. We watched in stunned amazement while they had sex on the rooftop. Holding hands across the table, our battle was over. We kept that nod of the chin, the iguana mating dance, as a personal symbol of our union.

In the cruising fleet, women ruled the social schedule. Our collective energy made college parties look like training sessions. Friendships formed quickly in response to the isolation created by being underway.

It was only 9:00 AM but dinghies were already being lowered into the water and the VHF buzzed like the party line it was. A haze hovered over the bay and boaters called each other, making plans to snorkel, locating a needed spare part, arranging shared rides to town and planning potlucks.

Crackling from the radio at our nav station came a familiar voice:

"*Nanook*, sailing vessel *Nanook*, this is *Circe*."

I scrambled down the companionway ladder and lifted the mike from its hook, pushed the button and replied. "*Hola, Circe*! This is *Nanook*, go to 19."

We made plans to meet on shore and take the bus to the marketplace. Barb from *Cherokee Rose* picked me up in her dinghy. Rick would need ours to take the laundry to the *lavanderia*.

Some evenings we rafted our dinghies together to watch a drive up movie on a television screen lashed to the cabin of an anchored boat. There were usually about a dozen of us on any given night, but on Valentine's Day the movie had been *Sleepless in Seattle* with two dozen of us rafted together. Everyone brought their own drinks and platters of snacks were passed between the boats. Rick and I stretched out on the floor of our dinghy using one of the inflated seats as a backrest. Covering ourselves with a light blanket, we prepared to watch a movie under the stars, while the water rocked the flotilla of dinghies.

About an hour into the movie the couple in the dinghy next to us yelped and sat upright. I looked over to see what the commotion was all about when a spray of water washed over us. "What the ..." I started to say. I thought a jokester was playing with an oar. Then I realized that it was dolphins flipping their tails. We turned our attention to the playful pranksters. Some were silent as submarines, circling and cruising just under our dinghies. They were so close I could hear air screeching through the holes in their snouts. They were gun metal gray on their topsides and lighter underneath. The performance of cartwheels and flips was a charming intermission and when they swam away, we all nestled back down to finish the movie.

When we'd been at anchor for two weeks, I wrote:

> It's time to go. We'll get underway early so we can cross Banderas Bay and round Cabo Corrientes before the morning winds kick-up. We'll make the overnight passage under the light of a full moon with boating pals within radio range.

The prospect of sailing at night with a light in the sky and the voices of Don and Sylvette from *Day by Day* within VHF radio range made leaving our neighborhood of friends less daunting.

DREAMING

Sometimes in the predawn hours
I slide in and out of sleep
and magic seems perfectly plausible.

Under a black umbrella
stars swim in silver.
Like the heavens above

all the places I want to touch
lie just out of reach

and our sailboat silently surfs.

> "If you reject the food, ignore the customs, fear the religion and avoid the people, you might better stay at home."
>
> JAMES MICHENER

CHAPTER 12
South to *Zihuatanejo*

I CRANKED THE winch handle, tightening the jib. The sun would be up in another hour. When the sail edge was no longer luffing, I was satisfied that it was neatly trimmed and we were getting full benefit from the wind. We were fifteen miles off shore, running parallel to the coast. *Nanook* jolted through the choppy waves like a car with four flat tires. We were jerking along at five knots. Feeling pretty proud of myself, I looked up at the sail and popped the winch handle out. It slipped; it flew; it disappeared.

On a sailboat, or at least on our boat, there seemed to be a rule: everything that wasn't tied down must jump into the sea. Tools had sought the briny deep and were followed by the barbecue grate, a dinner fork, leaving us with only five, and now an expensive winch handle. Nothing we dropped bounced inboard.

I didn't have time to pout because the windward jib sheet had snagged on the boarding ladder bracket. It was unbraiding; the wind shredded it while I stumbled forward to untangle the mess.

Exhaustion gripped me. I was stinky and in need of a bath. I was nursing a burned thumb from checking the oil at midnight. I wondered "What are we doing out here?"

The radar alarm sounded, jolting Rick awake. He stumbled into the cockpit. "What's up?"

"This is pure hell and Jimmy Buffett lies."

"Okay, I agree. But why is the alarm blaring?" Rick asked, looking for what new danger the radar had seen that we couldn't.

After a few minutes, we abandoned the troubleshooting and I went below, turned off the annoying alarm and opened a can of Trader Joe's stew. It was 5:00 AM when I plopped a double serving in a plastic bowl and went back to the cockpit. When the seas were this rough it was simpler to pass a single bowl back and forth than to set a proper table.

Between bites of tepid potatoes and mushy carrots, I said, "Remind me why we're living in this washing machine?"

Rick gripped the tiller between his legs and cradled the plastic stew bowl in his hands. "Can't remember, honey. I think ol' Jimmy crooned something about "Nibblin' on sponge cake and watchin' the sun bake." Rick danced in a pantomime version of "Margaritaville." "Searching for my lost shaker of salt."

I couldn't help laughing. The only thing salty was our encrusted skin.

We took turns being on watch, doing boat chores, reading and sleeping.

A little after 3:00 PM the VHF crackled and I reached for the microphone.

"*Nanook, Nanook*," the voice said. "This is *Hawkeye*."

"*Hawkeye*, good to hear from you. Go to 22?" I changed the channel and waited.

"*Hola, Nanook*. Are you there?"

"Yep, right here, John. Where are you?"

"I'm anchored and *Lucky Lady* is circling, ready to drop the hook. What's your ETA?"

"We're about an hour behind you. Is everybody still game for a potluck?"

"Sure thing. I'll bring cold beer."

"We're on our way. Out."

The five of us drank beer and scooped fresh salsa with *totopos*, homemade chips, in *Nanook*'s cockpit. The appetizers were courtesy of Judy. We had side-tied to *Lucky Lady*, Judy and Jay's forty-two–foot sloop. So, they only had to step over the lifelines to be on *Nanook*. The fifth was our friend John, a single-hand sailor on *Hawkeye,* anchored behind us.

I'd just put the food on the plates when an uninvited guest arrived. A twenty-foot bullet-gray inflatable pulled up to our stern. There were seven unsmiling uniformed men with machine guns staring at us.

"Permission to come aboard?" the tallest of the small men in uniforms asked, stepping over the life line. It wasn't a question. Three stayed in their boat and three followed him, their heavy boots making indentations in our seat cushions.

Nanook's cockpit was overcrowded with nine adults, four heavily armed and five armed with *cervesas*.

"*Hola*, we're having a party, *es una fiesta*." My jovial approach was wasted. These men had come to inspect our boat and wanted our boat papers.

Rick went below to get the files and three of the men followed. The leader stood at the galley counter, thumbing thoughtfully through our copies of crew lists and stamped entry and exit papers. I felt a surge of "this is going to be okay." I knew the documents were in order; we'd followed the rules and checked in with Immigration and Port Captains in every port with an office.

The best looking of the troop positioned himself at the foot of the stairs fingering his gun with a tight jaw line and a stance that screamed, "I'm serious about this." It would have been comical if it hadn't been intimidating.

The third and smallest, the one who was sweating so enthusiastically it looked as though we'd poured a beer on his head, waved his arms in a gesture that left no mistake in any language. I needed to start opening cupboards. Pointing at the settee, he said "*Abierto*" in a voice that was sweeter than I expected.

I lifted the cushion. Bad starting place. Neat piles of zip-locked bags of white powder stared back at us. Each was about the size of a pound of butter. Flour. Sugar. Salt. Cookie mix. Baking soda. I'd felt quite clever when I sealed them up two years ago in Long Beach. Now they screamed "cocaine" and our dinner guests were waiting.

I turned to look at the inspector but he'd already moved away. What was he looking for if he wasn't going to tear into these packets?

Back in the cockpit, I thought the entourage was leaving when their leader pointed at our guests. They weren't leaving until they'd checked their boats, too. *Lucky Lady* was side tied, so that was quick but *Hawkeye* was anchored 150 yards away. The looks on their faces, the language barrier and the size of their guns didn't lend themselves to discussing a compromise.

The uniforms hauled John into their boat, snapped a life jacket on him and roared away. John waved his hands over his head, pretending he was being kidnapped and calling, "Help me." We could hear him hollering, *"Ayúdame"* in jest. It was hilarious to us and I took his photo in the waning light. We probably shouldn't have made fun of foreign men brandishing weapons but sunshine and a happy attitude can be a wicked combination. The four of us waved our beers in a mock *adios* to John.

The officials returned him in less time than we expected and our party continued. The stroganoff was cold but our attitudes were chipper.

We sailed south for another full day and reached our destination, *Zihuatanejo*.

Rounding the corner of rocks at the entrance I drank in the sight of shore. My first impression was that we'd wandered onto the leading edge of a painting. At least a hundred sailboats tugged gently at their anchor lines.

They sat tall on a cobalt bay rimmed with a crystal surf line and a green fringe of palm trees. The thought occurred to me that we'd made a wrong turn and arrived in heaven. A wide swath of white sand shimmered in the sun. Magenta bougainvillea climbed the walls of sunflower yellow and chili red buildings dotting the hillsides.

It took nearly an hour to motor across the bay and choose a parking space. We didn't want to be too far from the beach with the least surf for dinghy landings and we needed plenty of room to swing on our anchor but we didn't want to be too close to shore where a bar might have noisy music at night. There was a lot to consider. While we circled, I stood on the bow and thought about never leaving.

I MET AN interesting lady named Bea. She and her husband had been cruisers in the late 1960s. He had since died and she was well into her 80s. They had sailed from San Francisco on a seventy-foot schooner. She had a car but didn't drive anymore so I took the keys and became her chauffeur for a couple of weeks. I enjoyed Bea's company and the independence of having access to a car. She regaled me with cruising stories that were thirty years old. She told me about teaching jobs at the American school and I wondered if staying in Mexico and getting jobs could be the next leg of our adventure? Bea said that the palatial homes on the bluffs just north of us were built with mafia drug money, that the boarding like the one we experienced with *Hawkeye* and *Lucky Lady* were training sessions for young military men. I believed her but I didn't know if it was true.

Wherever people congregate, communities seem to organize themselves and boaters are no exception. In alphabetical groups by boat name, we took turns cleaning the beaches, managing the radio Net and playing garbage scow in the anchorage. Art classes formed. Four of us started a writers group. One boat hosted sushi making classes and in another cockpit Spanish conversation classes convened. Restaurants in the village were meeting places for games of Bunco and dominoes and jewelry making.

One Sunday, there was an announcement from a *palapa* restaurant on the beach that they would tune their television from soccer to American football if enough cruisers showed up. That was U.S.-style marketing and it struck a chord. At the appointed time, at least sixty dinghies lined the long curved stretch of white sand. With our toes in the sand and beers on the tables, we settled in. Rick locked his eyes on the game. Mine wandered to the blue-gray mountains in the distance and emerald green palm fronds overhead. The broad thick leaves tapped a tune in the breeze.

Zihuatanejo is a special place so it made sense that cruisers honored her with a nickname. She was Z-town.

I learned to play Rummy cube and entered a tournament. The game is like a combination of gin rummy and scrabble and, while it took concentration, it was a good party game. I did the laundry while Rick was at the dentist. We had our film developed and I bought groceries. One month blended into the next.

With so many boats in the bay for a long time, the Mexican port officials figured, logically, that we must be dumping our holding tanks overboard. Back in the U.S. we'd hired companies like the "Honey Pot" to empty our holding tanks if we weren't at a marina dock that offered such a service. Cruising, we pumped our macerated poop directly overboard. And in bays where we anchored for periods of time beyond the capacity of our holding tanks, we pumped our sewage directly into the bay.

Zihuatanejo officials were on to us. It was the only port we visited where the officials announced on the VHF net that they were watching through binoculars. Those who didn't pull up anchor and motor out to sea every few weeks would be punished. We never heard what the punishment would be, but cruisers tend to be extremely thrifty and even a handful of pesos as a fine would be crushing. So, most of us took an occasional day sail to dump the tanks. Needing to leave had the benefit of re-arranging the parking lot.

Cruising is a little like high school; cliques form. Those with like interests or boat style tended to seek each other out. Boaters with equal-size wallets hung together. Sailors with similar backgrounds or interests became tight pals and the newbies, freshmen who didn't usually mingle with the old salts, kept to themselves as a novice class. All that changed in Z-town. The presence of a couple hundred boats blended the groups. I liked that.

An all-fleet potluck was held at the south end of the bay on a wide expanse of sand with enough space for volleyball. For those who wanted a different kind of exercise, there was a hike to a nearby lighthouse. But simply sitting in the sand with a margarita in hand and watching the dinghy landings was the best entertainment. The talented, lucky and boring caught the right size wave and rode it expertly, arriving dry and smug. The rest of the fleet performed circus tricks, getting caught sideways in a trough and sloshing their way to shore. Three dumped their passengers in the shallow water and were candidates for *America's Funniest Home Videos*, except we were just a bit south of the States and we didn't have television.

Snorkeling in the shallow waters off the beach, we saw pale blue sponges, peach-colored coral and fish in all the colors of a rainbow. I wore gloves when I snorkeled but I foolishly poked an urchin and the needle pricked my finger. It's not a good idea to swim in the ocean when you're bleeding, so I got out.

The temperature of the water and air in Z-town in the winter were a steady eighty degrees. It wasn't unpleasant duty to scrub *Nanook*'s water line using snorkel gear. I did the top three feet and Rick did the lower portion with scuba gear.

The most picturesque angle for a view was from the

patio at Puerto Mio. It was expensive by cruiser standards, but it was our seventeenth wedding anniversary. We got as dressed up as we knew how. A gauzy skirt and blouse for me, a clean and collared shirt and hand-pressed shorts for Rick. We tied the dinghy to a tree, rinsed our feet, put on sandals and walked. Past the Pemex station was a rickety bridge. Another half mile of rutted road brought us to the small elegant hotel with a bar overlooking the private bay.

Our place settings glowed in the waning light and the heavily starched napkins had been folded into complicated shapes. A barefoot waiter leapt over the rocks lighting lanterns tucked into crevices. We held hands and the moon sparkled on the water.

A white-clad waiter, looking as if he belonged on a cruise ship, took our order. We enjoyed margaritas, cold avocado soup and grilled fresh tuna steaks. Between bites of crème brûlée topped with crisp burnt sugar and sips of aromatic dark coffee, Rick handed me a small wrapped package. It was a ceramic cream pitcher painted in an intricate design of vivid blues and yellow by a local artisan. Owning something breakable was a treat and I hugged him with such enthusiasm that an observer might have thought he'd given me a massive diamond ring or a tennis bracelet.

We listened to the lap of the water against the rocks and the murmur of voices. A couple seated near us was admiring the sailboats in the bay. From the way they were dressed, we guessed they were staying at the hotel. We'd been like them once and probably would be again. For now, we weren't and that was good. Walking back to the dinghy we wondered if our table mates dreamed of sailing away.

Every few weeks a couple of boats announced their departure for the South Pacific. Part of me wanted to go, too, if not across the Pacific, then at least through the Panama Canal and into the Caribbean.

One morning, I was walking to my Spanish class with a throbbing head and a queasy stomach. I stopped and leaned against a post and then bent over double. I threw up in a planter box. It had to be unpleasant for the diners having breakfast at the nearby patio tables but when my stomach erupted I didn't have much choice. I wiped my face with a tissue and walked slowly back to the dinghy and out to the boat.

While I was lying on my bunk, a physician in the cruising fleet dinghied over to check on me. He suggested that Rick take a urine sample to a local lab. Rick left in the dinghy with the sample in a rinsed applesauce jar. Following the doctor's directions, he found the lab. A few hours and just eight US dollars later, we had the results and printed instructions. In English. Rick went to a pharmacy and bought antibiotics without a prescription. We marveled at the efficiency of such an uncomplicated, cheap and effective approach to medicine.

Tourists voiced nervousness about getting sick from eating lettuce, tomatoes, ice and whatever they'd been told might not be clean enough. The cruising fleet didn't dwell on any of the tourists' qualms. Most of what we ate was prepped in our own kitchens and we'd been in Mexico long enough to behave like locals. We ate off food carts and loved ice cream. We used the ice enthusiastically and didn't obsess about washing tomatoes and lettuce. Maybe being at sea made us as nervous as we could handle, which made food safety a non-event. Whatever the reason, we ate everything Mexico served and stayed pretty healthy.

My parents were arriving in a few days. They had reservations at a local hotel but we wanted them to spend some time on *Nanook*. The dinghy required agility so we motored out of *Zihuatanejo* Bay and into the nearby marina at *Ixtapa*.

The breezes in the bay had kept mosquitoes away but the marina didn't have enough air energy to move lint. Rick hung mosquito netting over the cockpit. It was also hotter in the marina without the ocean breeze and, of course, there was no pleasant rocking motion.

What we were missing was more than compensated for by the luxury of enormous tile bathrooms and wide concrete piers. Marina life meant no dinghy; our feet and fannies would be dry as long as we were marina rats.

Ixtapa is a village designed by the government to cater to Americans. Brand-name chain hotels and fast food restaurants lined the streets. Prices were high by cruiser standards but we had learned in *Cabo San Lucas* that American travelers in Mexico are willing to pay more for a hotel staff that spoke English and food and service that felt like they were in Seattle or Omaha instead of in Mexico. We were more comfortable with the real Mexico so I took the short bus ride into *Zihuatanejo* to shop.

One piece of luggage we'd asked my parents to bring was a large cardboard box full of boat parts. Some were for *KiaOra* and *Wildwind*; the rest were ours. Airport officials opened the box and examined its contents. We were used to the Mexican bureaucracy and took it in stride. Rick showed his tourist visa and Port Captain's authorization. They examined the contents and let us leave.

With my parents, we rode in taxis instead of on buses and ate in snazzier restaurants. But we also poked through the fresh food stalls and village *tiendas*. Mom and Dad were used to traveling and fit in well with our cruising friends. On their last night, I served grilled shrimp and rice in *Nanook*'s cockpit, handing the plates up two at a time. When I sat down, Mom said, "Christie, you make this all look so effortless, but it can't be. The dinner is delicious. And cloth napkins, too."

"Thanks, Mom," I replied. "This life is bringing out the best in me. I'm happy."

She hugged me. "I can tell, honey. But your father thinks that Rick should get back to work."

I patted her hand. "I understand."

We smiled at each other and went back to our dinner plates, accepting that we were on different planets regarding work and what constituted a worthwhile life.

Our friends, Dana and Jerry, visited, too. While Dana and I explored *Zihuatanejo*, Jerry swung in the hammock on *Nanook*'s bow.

"With an income of $200,000 I'd live this comfortably," he said over dinner one evening.

He was shocked when I said, "We're spending less than 10 percent of that."

Being landlocked in the marina created a different daily dynamic. With our visitors gone, we lounged by the swimming pool with the hotel guests. We showered in the marina's bathrooms and invested in citronella candles to ward off the pesky mosquitoes.

We were walking along the beach talking about our itinerary. North to *Mazatlan* and into the Sea of Cortez was one idea but south and through the Panama Canal was more appealing. So much hinged on whether the engine was dependable. Transiting big water and all the way to the South Pacific and Australia no longer appealed to us. There was just too much wind, water and trouble out there.

Hip deep in the surf, Rick cupped sea water in his hands and playfully threw a fistful at me. The sand was soft between my toes and I played in the water like a tourist. I was just waist deep but Rick dove into the waves and swam with strong strokes beyond the surf line.

I combed the sand for seashells and after no more than five minutes, I heard yelling and shaded my eyes, looking out to sea.

"Help, Help." Someone was waving and panic prickled my neck.

There wasn't anyone else out there. It was Rick.

"I can't get in," he called.

I was horrified and screamed, *"Ayúdame, ayúdame.* Help me! Help!" But the beach was suddenly empty of everyone but grandmothers carrying purses and very small children. Like a vision from a dream, a lone *panga* either heard me or saw one of us waving and circled back to Rick. He climbed into the boat and it roared off.

I walked back to the marina where I had to assume the boat was taking him, thinking, "All this talk about the dangers of falling overboard and I didn't have a boat when I needed one." I tipped the rescuer with a six-pack of beer, thinking "Rick's worth it."

A new arrival in the marina had sailed from New York and through the Panama Canal. Carol and Carl were headed north to California, so we traded navigation charts. Sailing south from *Huatulco* and across the Bay of *Tehuantepec* to transit the Panama Canal seemed feasible. We lovingly stored our new charts, certain that our engine would be dependable someday.

So the diesel became our top priority. Rick hired a fellow cruiser who made his living as a boat mechanic. He spent a few hours surfing in our engine room. He installed a vented loop that was supposed to fix the water in the oil problem as well as the overheating but the oil still looked like a milkshake. We committed ourselves to staying in the marina to see what we could do about it.

With the cockpit full of engine parts, it was time for a boat break. Even our black-and-white cow looked forlorn from her post on the aft railing. We took the bus to *Zihuatanejo* and walked across town to find the local bus to *Los Achiotes*. Our friends, Don and Judy on *Loon,* had told us that from there it was a short distance to *Barra de Potosí,* a beach facing the lagoon for fresh water swimming and a restaurant with hammocks.

Rural route bus drivers adorn the front of the buses to their tastes and this one was no exception. The windshield was framed with blue velvet fringe and tassels. Three CDs hung from the rear-view mirror. The CDs weren't for music, they were swinging prisms that sent rainbows of light across a large image of Mary and Joseph that hung behind the driver's head. The personalization of the bus always made me smile in contrast to an American bus where there not only would be no religious symbols but probably nothing unique, either.

If our driver hadn't stopped the bus and told us to get off, we wouldn't have known we'd arrived. We watched our bus rumble out of town. With beach bags over our shoulders, our intentions must have been obvious. Gestures and a few comprehensible words in Spanish from the locals on the street sent us to wait under a tree for *una camioneta*.

What had been described as a small bus was a pickup truck with rows of wooden benches. The back was piled with fish, scooped from the sea within the last few minutes. They were all less than a foot long and bright silver, giving the wriggling mass the look of gallons of boiling mercury. Three shirtless men wearing ragged blue jeans and thick-soled sandals scooped the fish into buckets.

When the truck was as empty of fish and as clean as it would be, one of the men imitated a gallant "your carriage awaits" with a flourish of his straw hat and a sweep of his arm. I climbed in and sat on a fish-scented plywood bench with my back to the cab of the truck. Rick sat next to me. The looks we gave each other said, "Seems okay, hope so."

We roared down the road leaving a trail of dust but stopped in less than two minutes. A dozen grade school children in crisp white shirts and tartan plaid uniforms scrambled in. We stopped again and a postcard salesman got on carrying his samples in a torn leather satchel.

We passed rows of identical houses freshly coated in pastel colors of tangerine, daisy, sky and grass. All boasted neatly raked dirt yards and spotless concrete walkways but we didn't see any evidence of running water or electricity.

The truck used the oncoming traffic lane to avoid tangles of dogs and pigs lying in the road. Chickens pecked the dirt and goats munched what little grass peeked out of the dust.

At every stop, a pair of the school kids climbed out of the truck and ran, giggling, toward one of the houses. Women carrying shopping bags climbed on and off. One man with a two-foot-tall green parrot perched on his baseball cap that had a San Diego Chargers logo between the hat's bill and the bird sat next to me. His head ornament's thick yellow beak was just inches from my cheek. I turned slowly and met the steely glare of a dime-sized black pupil ringed in neon orange.

I risked a smile at the image Rick and I must have made. We were two middle-aged Americans wearing flip-flops with brightly colored beach bags on our laps. We sat on fishy smelling planks in the bed of a pickup truck, surrounded by Mexican villagers going about their lives. We didn't know exactly where we were going but we were having an interesting time getting there.

When someone wanted to get out, they slapped the side of the truck and the driver stopped. It was all very genteel and quiet. After about thirty minutes, the crowd had dwindled to just the two of us again.

The air cooled and we could see the beach. A wooden sign read, *Barra de Potosí*. Rick slapped the side of the truck, looking quite smug that he'd caught on to the ways of the locals and we clambered out.

The white sand beach was the size of two football fields and faced a fresh-water lagoon with the ocean beyond. We chose a table and left our bags, jogging down to the water. We rinsed the travel dust from our faces and strolled along the beach. *Pangas* pulled high on the sand were filled with fishing gear.

At one of the *palapa* grills we chose a combination of abalone, oysters, shrimp and octopus. With cold drinks in hand we rested in our hammocks and waited for the food to arrive.

In the distance, a southbound cruising boat sailed by and we wondered if it was someone we knew, where they were going and if we would see them again. We hadn't brought our handheld VHF radio so we couldn't hail them to find out.

We spent the day eating and napping. The aroma of just caught fish frying on a wood fire mingled with the cadence of Mexican boom box music and my hammock swung to the syncopated drumbeat of the surf slapping the sand.

> *"We don't do these adventures to escape life, but to keep life from escaping us."*
>
> KAYAK JOURNAL ENTRY BY
> BRENT NIXON (JULY 2009)
> naturetalksbybrentnixon.com

CHAPTER 13

Exploring

WE GHOSTED INTO the bay under a thick blanket of humidity. Rick dropped the anchor and I furled the sails as the sky descended from dark to black. Once again, the setting sun had put on a spectacular show but we'd cut the timing too close for comfort.

The glowing ruby egg had made her curtain call as we approached the anchorage. We didn't like to make landfall after dark but neither did we want to spend another night taking turns on watch when we could be anchored and sleeping together.

Tired from the passage, we went to bed early and played footsie in our odd sleeping arrangement in the V-berth. After just a few hours of deep sleep I was wide awake, trembling. Rick seldom snored and the breathing I was hearing wasn't in sync with his. I shook his shoulder.

"Do you hear that?" I whispered.

"Yeah. Shh," he said.

Folding the sheet back, he sat up. I sat up, too. I could see in the darkness that he'd pulled the baseball bat out of hiding next to his mattress. Rick had brought the bat for protection because it was illegal to enter most ports with a gun onboard.

The sound of breathing somewhere in the boat had us holding ours.

With the club raised, in three strides Rick was at the ladder and I was right behind him. He stopped and I ran into him. It must have looked like a clip from a *Keystone Cops Meet I Love Lucy* show but we weren't laughing. The rumbling sound came from the cockpit. We climbed the stairs, Rick in front and me as close as his shadow. The heavy breathing was on our port side. We moved in that direction.

A lone whale lay next to *Nanook* as though we were rafted together. Her glistening back shone in the reflection of a pearl wedge of moon. She was as long as the boat.

Rick dropped the bat to his side and wrapped his arms around me. I leaned into his nakedness and we caressed each other, sighing. The whale continued its loud, rhythmic breathing and we stretched out on the cockpit cushions. There in the moonlight we made love with only the whale as a witness.

When the sun came up we saw that we were alone in the anchorage. The whale had gone and there were no other boats.

After coffee and a sponge bath we took the dinghy to shore and dragged it above the surf. The roller coaster ride left us salty and covered with sand from the waist down, but that wasn't unusual.

I heard the bus lumbering toward us. We boarded, gave the driver a handful of pesos and saw that all the seats were full. We stood in the aisle, my fist gripping a post. I was glad I'd left my jewelry in storage and was wearing a plain gold band. Being the only foreigners made me feel conspicuous enough. Even a small diamond had enough cash value to support everyone on the bus for at least a month, I thought.

Belching fumes, the bus coughed and hiccuped through a washed-out portion of road into a deep valley. Just when I thought we might end up walking, the bus limped up the cobbled roadway into town.

Mexican villages almost always have a *zócalo*, a square open space that is sometimes a grass park and more often paved and used as a community dance floor or basketball court. Today the *zócalo* had been converted to a supermarket. Mountains of bananas were piled in wheelbarrows. Open tables were filled with sweets and plastic toys. Hawkers hollering *camarones* scooped tiny shrimp into plastic bags with brown ice shavings in the bottom. They handed them out like snow cones in exchange for a few pesos.

We collected a bundle of mail at the stamp-sized post office. Every couple of months we called our forwarding service in Seattle and gave them the name of a post office where we thought we'd be. Within a few weeks, our name would be posted on the wall under the heading, *lista de correos*, which meant that they had mail for us.

A *taqueria* near the post office had an empty table so we ordered lemonade and ripped into the bulging white envelope, separating it into three piles. Important. Interesting. And trash, since recycle wasn't possible. There were letters from both girls.

On lined paper torn from a spiral notebook, AJ's left-handed chicken scratchings looked like Chinese characters. It took some deciphering, but the gist of it was that she was learning to speak Mandarin and trying to figure out what to do after graduation. She was double majoring in journalism and international relations. She closed the letter with, "I'm glad you've got this forwarding service 'cuz I've completely lost track of where you are."

Lisa's loopy scrawl was on a homemade card with the drawing of a boat on the front. She was doing her best to become an in-state student but she needed papers from us. She was frustrated that finding us was so complicated. I let out a sigh; getting the Notary stamp she needed was one of our errands for today.

We got a bill for the storage unit that held everything we owned that wasn't on the boat. An envelope from my parents included a four-color real estate flyer, photos of an elegant vacation home they had just purchased. Dad had written a note asking when we planned to return to the "real world." I thought about the meaning of "real."

Having a job, a house, a car? "Real" to me had come to mean making friends who were as unhurried as we were. "Real" meant eating what we caught and bartering what we didn't need for what we did. I wasn't quite sure how I would answer because our life on the boat was very real to us.

For an hour, mail connected us to the world we'd left behind.

We headed toward the town center, licking ice cream cones. Mine was melting fast and pink spots dripped on the envelopes and magazines cradled in my arm.

The first errand on our list was to get the form notarized for Northern Arizona University. The first two Notary offices we found were closed but at the third we learned that a Notary in Mexico is more like a lawyer. All we needed was someone to witness our signatures but Mexican Notaries apparently didn't do that. We improvised. Over fish tacos under a grass umbrella, we were venting our frustration at not being able to return the signed form. The fisherman who had cooked our tacos sat down at the table with a knife and a potato and carved out a reasonable-looking notary stamp. A few days later, a fellow cruiser produced an ink pad and I stamped the form twice, once with the potato and again with the bottom of a Corona bottle. We weren't sure what kind of scrutiny the document would receive at NAU, but we sent the fax and never got a reply.

We searched for a fly swatter, rubber cane stops to cushion the boarding ladder from the hull and size D batteries for our flashlight. These purchases were well beyond our command of the Spanish language so at each store we were reduced to gestures and drawings, an awkward but intriguing way to shop.

A man with a lined face the color of a walnut came toward us. He was hollering, "*Compra! Compra!*" and wore a leather sheath across his chest that held at least a dozen knives. We stepped aside to let him pass. He wore a sweat-stained sombrero, sandals with worn tire tread soles and tan long pants, frayed at the pockets and cuffs. In sharp contrast, his shirt was crisply ironed, a short-sleeved light blue dress shirt with an official emblem on the sleeve.

We watched him move through the shoppers, demonstrating the knives he was hawking and only when he was fifty yards past me did I realize what was so incongruous. I laughed out loud. Here was a Mexican man selling knives, wearing a United States Post Office shirt. The paradox of that shirt's journey through a web of thrift stores and donations to arrive in Mexico kept me chuckling.

Back on *Nanook*, the sea rippled with clouds of shrimp. It was my bathtub so I lowered myself into the water despite the presence of critters. Naked, I tread water and shampooed my hair. Tipping my head back to rinse, I thought about the palatial house my parents had just bought. No matter what home I ever lived in, I'd never have a master bathroom as sumptuous as the one I was using now.

I lay in my bunk with a laundry list of troubles parading. A bottle of liquid Joy had split, leaving a pile of yellow goo in the cupboard. Our solar panel contacts weren't charging the batteries. Rick had climbed the mast to tighten a bracket, dropped the pliers and they'd gone overboard. The autopilot was on the fritz. I'd repaired it before by taking it apart and putting scotch tape over the connections. It worked once, I'd try it again, I thought, dozing off to sleep.

I woke up to the sound of the bilge pump cranking. "Now what?" I muttered to no one. Rick wasn't in his bunk. I called, "I'm up, what's going on?"

"Stay in bed, honey. Galley pipe fitting's cracked. We'll have to use the sink in the head until we can buy a new part."

I crawled back into bed thinking about washing vegetables in the bathroom. A few weeks earlier, when the connection to the barbecue's propane hose failed while we were having a dinner party, I tossed the meat in the oven as if I'd planned it that way. These troubles were teaching me to be flexible, which was good, but I was tired of the constant challenge.

Mid-morning, we launched the dinghy and Rick rowed into the narrow fresh-water lagoon five hundred yards away. Dipping the oars silently, the only sound was the droplets of water falling from a raised oar before it sliced the water again. We whispered, passing within yards of cormorants, herons and hawks. Rounding a curve, I felt the movement before I heard it. With a whoosh of air, hundreds of white pelicans lifted off, squawking and chattering. The waterway was less than ten feet wide through most of the mangrove jungle and the canopy of interlocking tree branches created a tunnel that hid the sun.

We slipped through the lagoon for about an hour before we arrived at a clearing. There had been restaurants and houses at this site before an earthquake and tidal wave leveled them. We sat at a three-legged white plastic table that used a pile of coconuts as a fourth leg. A machete two feet long stuck from the trunk of a palm tree.

We ate grilled oysters, breaded octopus and, of course, fresh tortillas and beans. The families who served us slept on cots next to some bushes behind our table. There was a toilet that didn't have a flush system. I filled a bucket with water from the lagoon and poured into the toilet bowl, leaving it sort of ready for the next customer.

We wore shirts over our swimsuits and left them at the table. Wading into the water with our fins and masks on, we snorkeled in the shallow water. I held a piece of coral I'd found on the beach while I flutter kicked. Hummingbird-sized fish glowed like colored Christmas lights, swirling around me as if they were on a string. They teased my arms with butterfly kisses.

Standing on the deck after a night swim, bubbles of phosphorescence clung to my skin. Diamonds. I'd never been so glamorously attired. The comet Hyakutake shone in the north sky, a green searchlight beaming to earth. We kept meaning to leave but it was so peaceful, we stayed. For the next three weeks we explored the mangrove and ate at the makeshift restaurant. We fished. We cleaned the boat and did repairs. We read books and made love. We did the laundry and varnished teak.

I wrote in my journal:

> Life on the ocean is full of uncertainty. When the wind blows from the right direction it means a comfortable point of sail and a break from the noisy and unpredictable diesel. But rough seas and shifting winds can change all that, even in an anchorage.
>
> But I have everything I want. A devoted husband whose company I never grow tired of and the hours to enjoy each other. This ocean environment is our partner in the quest for an altered view.
>
> One realization is that life is better when it's harder. Food tastes better when it's scarce. When my father was a child, accumulation meant four dozen eggs instead of three, two bushels of apples instead of one. But that accumulation was because of an abundance on the farm and everything was put to good use. Accumulation in our lives had meant acquiring things that weren't necessary. It was stuff purchased in big box stores to replace things we already had.

That evening I was happy to hear a familiar voice on the VHF and to see a mast light at the entrance to the bay. *Timeless* had been in many of the same anchorages with us and we were pleased to see them now. They had refrigeration and shared a cold beer with us. We gave them fresh chunks of dorado to chill and enjoy and they gave us a chunk of ice.

After two days of playing on the beach, doing boat chores and sharing meals, they were ready to go. We said goodbye amidst chatter about seeing each other in another anchorage.

Boats came and went, some we knew and others were strangers who became friends.

There were four of us in the anchorage when the wind changed. It been calm until after midnight but now *Nanook* bucked like a rodeo bronco. Rick and I took turns on anchor watch while the wind pushed us toward shore. We ran the engine to take the pressure off the anchor. The bay was a washing machine in twenty-five knots of wind. We hadn't pulled the dinghy on board that night. It was bouncing wildly in the churning seas. In the dark, I ducked under the aft railing and tugged on the dinghy line to haul it in. I bumped my head on our little cow and she seemed to scowl at me.

The brass lantern twirled and the produce-filled hammock swung like a gymnast on parallel bars. The cabin was a steam bath and salt water seeped through the port holes, trickling in rivers onto the sofa. We played Mexican train dominoes and tried to ignore how close we were to the reef.

"Let me count the ways," I said to Rick in the beginning of a poetic-sounding moment that wasn't.

"I'm hot, wet, and miserable. We don't have refrigeration and our clothes are mildewing. Can you tell me why we're here? This time without the Jimmy Buffett impersonation, please, 'cause I'm convinced he never lived in 'Margaritaville.' I'm not getting the 'Good Vibrations' the Beach Boys crooned about either." By now, my hands were on my hips and I was shouting. I was wrung out with nothing left.

We talked on the radio with the other boats throughout the night and I clung to the security of their voices like a life raft. The biggest boat in the fleet dragged anchor and hit the reef at about 3:00 AM. There wasn't any major damage and he re-anchored farther out. The rest of us discussed pulling up anchor but decided against it. Equipping *Nanook* with two oversized anchors, we had enough ground tackle for a much larger boat. That was something we'd done right.

At 4:00 AM the radio crackled again.

"*Nanook, Nanook,* this is *Pacific High.* How ya' doin' over there? Over."

"*Hola,* Bev. We're bouncing around just like you guys but the anchor's holding so we're staying put. How 'bout you?"

"Ivan says it's time to go. We're pretty close to shore so we're pulling up anchor and wanted to say "Goodbye." We'll head out to sea and catch you in a few days."

"Well, you guys take care and stay in touch."

"Will do. Out."

In the days after the other boats left, we spent more time in the nude because we were alone. Rick installed the new engine hour meter that friends had delivered. He climbed the mast to fix the steaming light and together we carved some insulation off the ice box lid because it had swollen in the persistent humidity and no longer closed. Then Rick moved his focus to the engine room. We usually ran the diesel for a few hours a day to recharge the batteries but that was impossible with it dismantled and lying around the cockpit. We used power judiciously, turning the radios off when we weren't using them and not watching movies.

Our projects were interrupted by the sound of a motor. Rick called to me, "Honey, cover up, we've got company."

I slipped a long T-shirt over my head and climbed into the cockpit. Two young men on the twenty-four-foot sloop *Wanderlust* waved.

"Ahoy, *Nanookers*," they called.

They were strangers but had read our name on the stern. They anchored, dropped their dinghy and rowed over. They climbed aboard, carrying bottles of rum and coke. We had some ice left and chipped a few chunks from the block into plastic glasses.

Todd and John were firemen on an extended break from work. They were on a surfing expedition but had anchored in our quiet bay to explore the beach. Cruisers seldom share anchorages with surfers because the waves they ride aren't what a sailor seeks. To us, the sound of

crashing surf conjured an image of foaming fingers clutching us like a toothpick and tossing us onto the sand. A surfer's delight is not a pretty picture to a sailor.

John asked, "So, how long are you two out here?"

Rick explained that we didn't really have a timeline. Without jobs to return to and very low expenses we were keeping it flexible.

"Our original idea was to sail around the world," I chimed in but admitted that a circumnavigation looked doubtful.

They were envious and we explained that some places we stayed just one night because of flies, mosquitoes or a wind shift. Provisions dictated our plans, too. When we needed fresh water or diesel we chose a marina instead of an anchorage. We'd chosen this anchorage because cruising friends had told us that a bus came near the beach; we could flag it down and ride to town.

Todd said our lives sounded perfect and that he wanted to be married someday, to sail away. To live like we were.

I laughed. "Be careful what you wish for. *Nanook* is one of the smallest and least luxurious of the boats in the fleet." But to these two guys, we had it all.

"It seems as if all the wonderful women are in your generation, not ours," John said as they prepared to leave.

I felt motherly and told the young men. "Just be patient, we're out there. Women say that all the good guys are gone, too. Then Rick showed up." He patted my rear end in a gesture of agreement and applause.

The guys rowed away.

Rick put his arm around me and said, "Life is as unpredictable as sailing. You date, marry – in our cases the wrong person. Then, when you don't expect it, bingo. The right partner appears and, as the T-shirt says, 'Life is good.'" He kissed my forehead.

> *"It is not length of life, but depth of life."*
> RALPH WALDO EMERSON

CHAPTER 14
Spice and Spirit

My string bags were in my pockets. I landed the dinghy on the beach and struck out on foot in search of the marketplace.

First were fruits and vegetables in brilliant greens, vibrant yellows, rustic reds and fall orange. Avocados were piled next to chiles, dried bunches hanging in swags. The scene begged for watercolors and brushes, or at least a flash camera.

Red and yellow bananas from three inches to almost a foot long were stacked next to plump limes. Just looking at them I could taste their tart rain in a beer or drizzled on fresh fish.

Papaya and pineapple thickened the air with sweetness; pyramids of mangos had a stunning symmetry. Despite the darkness inside the roofed marketplace, it smelled like sunshine.

Pearls of rice glowed in baskets lined with a rainbow of cloths. I was enchanted.

Children took orders from customers and gave change. Language surged around me and I floated on it, like riding a wave. Mothers in striped serapes with babies wrapped on their bellies supervised and nursed the little ones. Whole coffee beans overflowed from brown glazed ceramic pots and the nutty aroma offered its "good morning" benediction.

The rows of tables extended the length of a football field and were arranged as if an artist had designed it for show. Shoppers clustered in front of the long rows of stalls; elbow to elbow they tasted, touched and sniffed before buying. Shopping was an active sport and I was in love. It was a visceral experience. No product packaging. No bar codes. No shopping carts.

I followed my nose to a black kettle the size of a bathtub resting on an open wood fire.

A short man, with a face so deeply lined it looked as if there were pockets carved in his cheeks, stirred the pot with a four-foot paddle. Another rhythmically macerated tomatoes on a scarred wooden board using a large machete. He used the blade to shove the wet, red mass into the pot. Onions diced to resemble hail stones drifted over the tomatoes. Fresh cilantro, snipped and clipped, scattered like flower petals over the top. The mixture was tantalizing.

The surge of shoppers shifted to make room for a burly man with the carcass of a cow slung over his head, a white tea towel covering his hair. A line of customers followed him and I did, too. I passed a row of skinned goats hanging by their hooves, horns still attached. The air smelled of warm blood and flies swarmed.

I found myself in a cluster of shoppers, stopped at a marble slab where freshly slaughtered pigs and cows hung on hooks. When the customer had selected the beast she wanted, the butcher released a rope, dropping it six feet lower so he could whack off a hunk to the shopper's satisfaction. The butchers sharpened their knives and cleaved with the energy of a percussion band, the rhythm creating its own energy. The stench of blood and warm meat was thick in the air. I got in line. When it was my turn at the counter, I asked the butcher to carve a chunk of steak. He held up two fingers, asking what thickness I wanted. I used my thumb and index finger in reply. I placed the beef steaks, double bagged with ice shavings, in the bottom of my shoulder bag and moved on.

On the outside edge of the market I found a chicken vendor, a woman wearing a long dress and sandals. I asked for *dos pechugas sin huesos* (boneless breasts). She turned to a boy who couldn't have been older than eight and her rapid Spanish sent him scurrying. I heard squawking, followed by the blur of the small boy's red shirt in rapid pursuit. Within five minutes, I handed over a few pesos and got my two boneless chicken breasts. Warm and fresh.

A cluster of shoppers converged in front of a stall

where a man wearing a crushed straw hat was selling a sauce I didn't recognize. On a yellow oilcloth, two women chopped green and red *chiles*. A young boy used a dirty fingernail to scrape the pale seeds into a bucket. The fire threw its sparks when a youngster poked it with a stick. One end of the table was covered with piles of peanuts, almonds and raisins. A woman expertly massaged a knife up and down, pulverizing the mounds into fine dust. I leaned close to sniff an ingredient I didn't recognize. The familiar aroma told me it was cloves. With meaty hands the man in the hat alternately dropped coins in his apron pocket and passed his customers small plastic bags filled with brown paste. The goo was the consistency of thick gravy and smelled like onions and chocolate. The combination rang bells of conflict to my North American taste buds but I had decided long ago that connection requires participation so I exchanged three pesos for a small bag of the brew.

I held it aloft and asked, "*Qué es esto?*" Being blunt had worked in the past and was necessary with my limited Spanish vocabulary.

"*Es mole.*"

The sauce is indigenous to the *Oaxaca* region of Mexico and I had read that families have their own mole recipes that are part of their genetic footprint. Each family uses different ingredients and guards the secret.

I smiled, holding the bag to my nose again and inhaling deeply. "*Me parece muy sabroso.*" and it was delicious. That night we dunked bites of grilled chicken breast into the mole sauce, licking every drop from our spoons and plates.

In the fish market I bought *camarones*, shrimp that had been scooped from the sea in the last few hours. The fishermen bagged them in ice shavings and I worked my way through the crowd, deeper into the mass of stalls.

I made my choices, bargaining for the quantities I thought we could use, and moved through the pulsing throng. Herbs in brilliant bunches filled the air with their individual scents. In separate cubicles, I bought a jicama and a handful of tomatillos.

My nose took me to some unwrapped bars of soap. The smell collided with the aroma of food but I bought one, hoping it would lather up. The only thing I'd found so far that worked in salt water was Joy liquid dish soap and I longed for the tradition of a bar of soap in my bath.

Next to the soap table, a woman scaled needles from a cholla cactus with a massive knife. We had tasted a delicious nopales salad made with diced cactus ears, pine nuts and raisins and I wanted to see if I could duplicate it. She gave me a toothless smile when I raised my index finger. Her pace didn't change and the pile of spike-less cactus paddles grew faster than I could pluck a few pesos from my pocket.

"*Solamente uno?*" She looked at me as if I'd lost my mind. I suppose asking for just one was like wanting a handful of coffee beans. She handed me the lone cactus ear, waving her hand in a gesture that said, "*Gratis.*"

My tiny purchase wasn't worth enough to charge even a peso.

"*Muchas gracias,*" I smiled, a little embarrassed and handed the few coins to a little girl running by.

My cactus salad recipe called for skinning and boiling the chubby leaf, pressing all the moisture out and dicing the leathery meat. It was a failed experiment when the cactus boiled and turned to jelly. I didn't buy any more cactus.

The line in front of the *tortilleria* was long. Women, young and old, chatted amiably and the line inched forward. I admired their visible patience doing mundane errands. It was a scene repeated in every town we visited. Teens wore skin-tight jeans and the tots holding their hands, crisply ironed shirts. The dresses of their elders fit the description of what my grandmother called "house dresses" in the 1950s. Floral prints in pastel shades hung to the calf, the fabric lifting like laundry in the breeze. All ages stood in line with an assortment of wicker baskets and plastic buckets slung over their arms.

Leaving the counter with their warm tortillas draped with a piece of cloth, they moved quickly, losing the lethargy of line standing. Watching, I imagined a sturdy table set for the midday meal. Three or four generations of family members, roasted chicken, beans, rice, and vegetables were waiting for the arrival of the tortillas.

I didn't buy tortillas because I'd learned that if we didn't eat them within an hour or two they turned into hard platters, frisbees to toss at the seagulls.

And I never saw any adult men in the tortilla lines. Men fished and worked in the fields. They staffed the government offices, carved meats, and played checkers. They sold goods but they didn't visibly shop. Women's work was a separate deity.

IT WAS NOVEMBER and the cruising community had bonded with a common goal: the creation of a traditional American Thanksgiving. I questioned our sanity. All these delicious foods in the Mexican markets were being ignored and our friends were enthusiastically trying to duplicate a traditional American banquet. I preferred Mexican *machaca* to cornbread stuffing but it appeared I was alone in my lack of enthusiasm for finding turkeys in Mexico.

Our first Thanksgiving had been soon after we left *Isla Guadalupe*. There, on the west coast of the Baja, we had sat on towels in the coarse sand and shared a festive picnic with three other couples. We had worn swimsuits and dined on teacup-sized scallops roasted in garlic butter. Hoisting a plastic fork, I had toasted the absence of turkey and tradition. One of the boats had caught a wahoo. They served it four ways: presented on a platter the huge fish had been grilled, stuffed, poached in coconut juice and fried crisp with lime wedges. Each of us had contributed and our holiday picnic included a pork roast, yams, carrots, muffins, mango salad, and cookies.

Now we found ourselves in the middle of a network of cruisers planning a traditional Thanksgiving dinner. In Mexico. I couldn't figure out what motivated them to go to such great lengths to duplicate the lives we had all left on purpose.

The morning Net was full of details about assembling enough tables and chairs. Guests arriving by airplane had been asked to pack canned cranberry sauce, boxed stuffing or wild rice in their suitcases. Frozen turkeys were transported like bowling balls in carry-on luggage.

In every galley, first mates were trying to create reasonable facsimiles of a traditional Thanksgiving. Not wanting to be a poor sport, I scrounged the back corners of our food lockers and baked a cranberry cake and a pumpkin pie.

A pair of cruisers from Texas marinated turkeys in Tabasco. I had no idea that hot sauce came in large enough bottles to fill the fifty-gallon ice chests. The largest size I'd ever seen was smaller than a tube of travel-sized toothpaste but I'm not from Cajun country.

We assembled on the spacious lawn of a former cruiser who had bought a condo overlooking a lagoon. The turkeys bubbled in propane-fired deep fryers. Cruisers who'd been sailing the longest had used up their original provisions and created more Mexican-style offerings. That meant pickled octopus, cactus salad, and *manchego* cheese platters.

We brought our own plates, so I filled mine with hearts of palm, smoked tuna, sweet potatoes, stuffing, and gravy. And Cajun turkey was the tastiest I'd ever eaten.

> *"Ask and it shall be given you; seek and ye shall find; knock and it shall be opened unto you."*
>
> MATTHEW 7:8

CHAPTER 15

Navidad

A LIGHT BREEZE lifted my hair in the anchorage and the sea slapped the hull in a rhythmic motion. It was December 23. Our third Christmas at sea. The tropical tranquility that surrounded us bore none of the snow globe images that signaled the season. The music on the CD was about snowflakes and brought images of square-paned windows and candles flickering on their sills.

Rick clipped socks to *Nanook*'s lifelines with clothespins, not as laundry, but to create a Christmas scene. I decorated a palm frond with tiny seashells, tucking it between books so our makeshift Christmas tree wouldn't topple over as we rocked. The sky darkened from orange to purple and the bay was a thousand yards of dark blue velvet.

In the warm night air, with visions of reindeer in our heads, we watched dolphins splash. They played with our stern anchor line. Two little ones used the line like a jump rope. Three more took turns scratching their backs on the line's tough braid. Back and forth they went, looking so satisfied we could almost hear them moan. The vibrating anchor line resonated like a tuning fork.

Kneeling over the stern railing, I watched the largest dolphin just a few feet away. Fixing one bright eye on me, he rocked his silver snout in time with the music.

I called to Rick, "Honey, come see this. Our dolphin knows the iguana mating dance."

In two strides Rick crossed the cockpit and put his hands on my shoulders. The dolphin slapped a fin on the surface, spraying us with salt water before he rocked his head back and made chattering noises. He might have been gurgling in dolphin squeaks, but it sounded like "Merry Christmas" to me.

The next morning we lowered the dinghy into the water and motored to shore. Just ten weeks earlier, there had been a devastating earthquake near here. When the ground stopped shuddering and the aftershocks began, the waters of *Bahía de Navidad* roared out of the bay, into the Pacific Ocean and then returned, a monster the height of a two-story building. We wanted to see how the village had recovered, to re-provision with fresh fruit and vegetables and to buy each other a Christmas present or two.

We pulled the inflatable across the sand and tied it to a palm tree. A cluster of children played in the sand with the pottery characters from a crèche. Slabs of concrete lay at odd angles where the streets had buckled and buildings caved in. Navigating the chunks of disconnected walls that protruded from what had recently been beach-side storefronts, we walked into town.

A row of palm trees along the main street slumped like weary soldiers home from a war. Someone had draped strings of holiday tinsel from their fronds and red bows hugged their trunks. The air was ripe with the matching scents of salt and just-caught fish.

Tables had been set up, creating the atmosphere of a Christmas bazaar. Vendors hawked their wares and shoppers bartered. A group of children shared a cardboard box in the dirt road. It became a wagon, a drum and then a sled as the games changed.

A fine dust powdered my shoes and I felt centuries removed from *Las Hadas* and *Manzanilla*, the nearest tourist meccas. We followed the sound of clapping and entered the dimly lit adobe building where a woman slapped corn dough into saucer shapes and tossed them on a grill. We sat down and lunched on grilled spicy meats topped with white crumbled cheese. Accompanied by black beans, red salsa, warm corn tortillas and fried plantains, it was a satisfying Christmas Eve brunch.

Outside, a dog lay in the dusty road, looking more like a dirty bag of hardware than a pet. One after another, heavy-set women wearing flowered dresses with skirts that moved in the breeze walked serenely past. All carried baskets on their heads; whether tortillas or laundry, the bundles were balanced on top of dark shiny hair.

One section of stalls displayed an array of goods reminiscent of a United States dime store decades ago. Brands we remembered had resurfaced. Perfume with faded labels. Boxes of hula hoops. Brooms in every conceivable size and color stuck out of buckets. Cellophane-wrapped board games and dusty boxes of Christmas lights were on tables next to men hawking whole fish and chickens, sides of beef, kitchen tools and shiny shoes.

I bought a tube of toothpaste, a jar of skin cream and a bottle of shampoo. Rick picked out ripe avocados and plump limes. Pastries that resembled a baseball glove were draped with cloths in a futile attempt to discourage the flies that were everywhere.

I stopped at a cart displaying fresh fruit on sticks, the dripping slices of mango and papaya piled high. I put down my packages, wrestling my camera from the bottom of my bag. We negotiated for a block of ice to be delivered to our dinghy and filled five-gallon jugs with fresh water to add to our tanks on board. We separated to buy

 Christmas presents for each other and agreed to meet at the dinghy.

IT WAS 2:00 in the morning when we were awakened by a noise. We looked at each other with curiosity but not alarm.

"What's that?" I asked.

"I have no idea." Rick answered, sitting up. He put his hand through the hatch to see if it might be rain, which it wasn't. I dismissed the fanciful notion it could be Santa's reindeer and we crawled out of the V-berth to investigate.

Standing in the cockpit we laughed out loud. Fish were jumping. Split, splat. By the hundreds they broke the glassy surface. The sea was a mass of miniature Tivoli Garden fountains surrounding us. Each one glowed with a sparkler-sized trail of phosphorescence. The surface of *Bahía de Navidad* glowed in the early hours of Christmas morning.

We went back to bed and got up at a more reasonable hour. I kneaded dough for Christmas muffins and

Rick rinsed hundreds of tiny fish from the decks. Sipping coffee in the cockpit, we watched the dough, mixed with walnuts and cranberries, rise in the warm sunshine on the cabin's rooftop.

"You look deep in thought, honey, any specific Christmas-past you're revisiting?" Rick asked, setting his coffee cup down and turning toward me.

I smiled. "That transparent, huh? I was just thinking about the girls and what they're doing today."

"My guess is that AJ's fine and hardly noticing it's Christmas and that Lisa's missing us badly. You mostly. It's been harder on her having you gone; no house to go home to on school breaks and all that."

"I'm sure you're right. I love what we're doing but it would have been easier for Lisa if we'd been more conventional and stayed home."

We were quiet with our own thoughts. Rick broke the silence with a chuckle, "Lots of proverbial water over the dam since our first Christmas together," he said.

"That's for sure; they were just little girls and now they're almost grown up. Takes a lot less wrapping paper and scotch tape now," I said before I turned serious again. "I just hope they aren't sad today. I can't even begin to picture what AJ's doing in China but it hurts to picture Lisa alone in her apartment and working at the movie theatre this afternoon…" my voice trailed off.

"Try not to worry, sweetie. You and I've had some sad holidays during our growing years and we survived," he patted my hand. "Hey, just look at us now," he gestured toward the shoreline, surveying the idyllic setting where we were anchored.

"I know, you're right. But once a mom always a mom. I can't just turn my worry meter off."

He stood, kissed the top of my head and went below, returning with our wrapped packages. Rick gave me the bottle of cologne he'd bought the day before and I gave him a local brand of tequila that we hadn't tried.

I set our cockpit table with straw placemats and festive napkins tied with raffia. In the center of the table I carefully set the blue-and-yellow cream pitcher Rick had given me for our anniversary. I filled it with Mexican crema, a white sauce that we poured over our omelets.

In late afternoon, after siestas, we went ashore and took a thirty-minute bus ride to the village that had been the epicenter of the quake. Scratchy strains of recorded Christmas music drifted into the street. The only other sound was the distant cadence of waves on the beach and the voices of neighbors going about their daily routines.

A restaurant had set up tables in the alley and we sat down at one of them. Chickens that would be dinner by nightfall pecked the ground at our feet.

With her pony tail bouncing, a skinny young girl who couldn't have been older than six put a basket of chips and bowl of salsa in front of us. We asked for two cold lemonades. A little boy, a mirror image of his sister, put the ice-cold drinks in front of us within minutes.

Four men in white shirts and bow ties appeared. The

guitar player asked, "*Quieres un cancion?*" We really didn't but music was what they were selling so Rick said, "*Como no?*" For a few pesos they serenaded us with a half dozen familiar Christmas carols, in Spanish. The children sang along, and the little girl climbed onto Rick's lap.

I sang quietly, in English, wondering how the shortest of our serenaders managed to carry his huge bass guitar. When they finished, he lifted the instrument and moved gracefully down the street with an ease that indicated decades of experience.

A family trooped by and sat down at a long table. I counted. Two babies in their mothers' arms, a man hunched over and using a cane, four school-age children, two toddlers and three handsome men who took their straw hats off as they passed, dusting them on their black pants. They wished us "*Feliz Navidad*" and we replied, "*Igualmente.*"

I reached under the table for the Santa's bag of treats that Rick and I had brought for this purpose. It was Christmas day in *Cihuatlán* and the gifts bulged from our bright blue laundry bag that Rick had been carrying over his shoulder. Inside were packets of wrapped candy, small boxes of crayons, tablets of paper, tubes of bright lipstick, individually wrapped cigars, toothbrushes and plastic checker sets. We also had glorious hair bows on clips to give away. Just before we'd set sail, my brother's daughter had cut her long hair and sent us the dozens of hair bows she no longer needed.

I motioned for the children to come closer while Rick

loosened the bag's white drawstring. The tiniest toddler got there first. She was dressed in red velvet and her brother, missing his two front teeth, was right behind her. They peeked in the mystery bag. I reassured their parents. *"Estamos Americanos,"* I said, as if that wasn't obvious. *"Bibemos en un barco de vela"* and *"tenemos regalos"* explaining that we lived nearby on a sailboat and that these were our gifts to them.

The children poked in the bag, laying the gifts on our table before they made their choices. They scurried between the tables like Santa's elves. The little ones who seemed to live there joined in, carrying gifts for their parents through the door behind us.

When we finished our lemonade, we walked down the street, the blue Santa's bag, embroidered with *Nanook* in white cursive lettering, hanging over Rick's shoulder.

A plump woman in a print dress rearranged the dust of decades with her broom. The scraping sound had a centuries-old beat, the pulse of the town. We passed a cluster of men playing checkers. We moved slowly, putting the bag down to pull out gifts for everyone we passed.

After a few blocks, children grew bolder, approaching us and asking to look inside the magic bag. With our encouragement, they helped themselves to presents for their siblings and parents as well as themselves. After more than an hour, most of our gifts were gone and we were ready to head back to the boat.

In the fading sunlight, we headed for the bus stop. Rounding a corner, we heard voices and saw candles flickering. We watched the procession. About thirty villagers of all ages walked by, chatting quietly, carrying lighted candles. We turned and joined in, the only white faces in the growing parade.

A matronly woman walked next to me, holding the hand of a thin man, both dressed in freshly pressed Sunday best. The family from the restaurant nodded in recognition. A short, sturdy *abuela* handed Rick two candles.

Neighbors chatted with each other, submerging us in language that was beyond our understanding. It was like standing in the orchestra pit at a jazz concert. There was melody and energy, a cacophony of blended sounds, but without recognizable words. Because I couldn't comprehend, I built my own interpretation of the layers of stories being told around me. Like a warm blanket, it was comforting.

The procession snaked through town on the cobblestone roads and villagers continued to join the surging assemblage until we came to a stop at the top of a hill. Young mothers with children on their hips, backs and in their arms grew silent. A giggling group of pre-teens waved their candles wildly until they were hushed by a middle-aged man waving his straw hat at them in a motion that spoke louder than words.

Three children approached us, smiling shyly as they reached into the blue Santa bag of gifts, selecting the last of our gifts. In reverent silence we stood near the entry of the temporary chapel that had been set up between the earthquake-toppled church buildings. Hundreds of candles flickered, illuminating the white stucco church spire. The cracks in the walls were large enough for sea birds to fly through.

The grandmotherly looking *abuela* who had given us our candles stood close to me. I'm just 5 foot 2, but she was no taller than my shoulder. Her face was like a well-worn leather wallet and she was dressed entirely in black, from the knitted shawl that covered her head to her scuffed shoes. She leaned on a cane roughly whittled from a tree branch, her eyes focused on the crucifix on the makeshift altar.

Without turning her head, she spoke in rapid Spanish. When I didn't respond, she lifted her chin in my direction, gesturing toward the cross. I shrugged, motioning with my hands that I didn't understand. My limited study of Spanish wasn't enough. Her smile deepened the pleats around her mouth. Her dark eyes sought and held the gaze of my blue eyes. She reached up and patted the empty gift bag.

She couldn't tell me her story and I couldn't tell her mine, but our hands clasped and we spoke without words. With neither a common culture nor language, we communicated.

> *"There is nothing like returning to a place that remains unchanged to find the ways in which you yourself have altered."*
>
> NELSON MANDELA

CHAPTER 16
Going Home

MEXICAN LAW REQUIRES visitors to have valid travel visas. It's a form easily filled out by vacationers on the airplane without giving it much thought. They write the dates of their vacation, which is usually two to three weeks. The fact that the maximum allowed is six months posed a complication for us.

We kept our visas valid in a variety of ways. If we had visitors coming, we asked them to pull a couple of extra forms from the tablet. Once, we took a bus across Mexico to Texas and re-entered at Ojinaga. Every trip outside Mexico started a fresh six months of legal residency.

Needing new visas now, we flew to Los Angeles, rented a car and stayed for two weeks. AJ had graduated from Boston University and was living in Shanghai so we didn't get to see her but we spent a good week with

Lisa, catching up on news and having conversations longer than a phone call.

We were staying with my parents and when my mother introduced me to her friends at the country club, the phrase that most often followed "It's nice to meet you" was "Where are you from?" It's a simple question if your life is normal, which mine wasn't, especially in a roomful of people with multiple homes, one for each season. My homelessness was not only odd, but suspect.

I tried the truth, "We travel full time and don't really have a home right now." If that didn't make them turn their attention to someone more normal, I explained, "My home is a sailboat." That reply often struck a responsive chord among men, but women skated away in search of someone more conventional. With practice, I honed a neutral response that was better received. "We're from Oregon," I'd say with a lukewarm smile. It was partially true. We had lived there, might return someday and we had Oregon driver's licenses. After two weeks of answering the "where are you from" question, I recognized a truth: my home was wherever my stuff was.

Two cruising couples visited while we were at my parents' home. Giving them the tour, with wine glasses in hand, we stopped to chat in the guest bedroom closet. It was larger than *Nanook*.

We were scheduled to be the guest speakers at the monthly meeting of Power Squadron, the same folks who had chuckled in amusement when we said we were going to buy a boat and sail around the world. So, we said our goodbyes to family and loaded a borrowed slide projector into our rental car.

They called the meeting to order and I looked out at the sea of familiar faces. Many of these veteran sailors dreamed of sailing away but didn't. We were the Nikes in the crowd, the ones with the "Just do it" spirit.

Rick turned on the slide projector and we took turns telling the story behind the pictures. They listened with rapt attention to our stories about eating what we caught, collecting seashells, scrounging spare parts and learning as we sailed. Packing the box of slides in the car, I said to Rick. "Isn't it amazing that we're experienced enough to teach our teachers?"

"You know, I was thinking the same thing. They're still meeting in that same room and we've been in Mexico for three years," he replied, closing the trunk.

In the morning, we continued to San Diego, stopping at marine and engine parts stores, our boat insurance agent's office and finally at the Mexican government office for new visas.

A month earlier, we'd been excited about returning "home" to the United States. We'd looked forward to the familiar language, stores and habits. Now we only wanted to be back in Mexico, to the charm of an unhurried pace where shopping was a scavenger hunt instead of a supermarket sweep. We'd seen Lisa and that was good but we missed *Nanook* and our cruising lives.

We ditched the last half of our "To Do" list along with our plans to spend the night in a San Diego motel.

Rick parked the rental car on the U.S. side and we walked across the border.

Mexican bus schedules are posted on the wall, listing times and prices for each leg of the journey, but never for the entire trip. If the schedule read this way in the U.S., going from Seattle to Los Angeles would mean buying a ticket in Seattle to Olympia, then to Portland, in Portland to Eugene and continuing southward one ticket at a time. A good map helps if the traveler isn't acquainted with all the little village stops en-route. For a pre-planning American it's a leap of faith.

By the good fortune of the travel gods, we met Xavier, a Mexican taxi driver. For a flat fee he would ferry us and our gear from the border, through customs and to the bus station. He left us at a taco stand, agreeing to return as soon as possible. Using simple English and a little Spanish, we understood that he wasn't allowed to take passengers into the United States in his taxi so he was going home to get a different car.

Mexican life is far from luxurious but everyone looked happy going about their daily routines. By contrast, Californians had looked grim driving their luxury cars, miserable while shopping in air-conditioned comfort and annoyed dining in spotless restaurants.

Rick and I talked about what it was that had bothered us about being in the United States. Our dissatisfaction and confusion were hard to identify while we were in the throes of family visits. With a few hours' distance, we saw a pattern to our distress.

Visible excess led the list: big box stores where impersonal shopping was the trademark. Acres of storage units dotting the landscape because Americans owned more than they could store in their huge homes and garages.

In a sprawling supermarket I was overcome by the sight of pristine shelves lined with fifteen kinds of mustard, the display taking up yards of shelf space. Plastic, glass and squeeze bottles of Grey Poupon, yellow with onion bits, organic wild mustard and more. In Mexico, when I had found a jar of mustard in a *tienda*, I snatched it like a child with a favorite doll despite its dented and dirty lid. We used it sparingly, uncertain when we would find a replacement.

Buying meat that was cut and carved in front of us, with flies and blood being part of the picture, was what we were used to. Cows, chickens and pigs walked to the market and left filleted in plastic bags on ice chips. I'd grown up with bloodless rows of Styrofoam meats sealed in shrink-wrap, but now I preferred the Mexican way.

I liked buying sun-ripened papayas and lemons with a powerful citrus scent that lingered on my hands. In America we were dismayed at the array of supermarket fruits that looked perfect but didn't have any flavor. Baseball-hard products probably survive being boxed and shipped better than ripened fruit, but we missed the vegetable vendors with products that smelled like what they were.

We munched on authentic Mexican tacos, squeezing lime into cool Coronas and licking the sweet juice from our fingers. The day was bright and sunny; the music of the language engulfed us.

Xavier returned and drove us across the border to our rental car. We loaded three duffle bags, two canvas bags, golf clubs and four boxes of different sizes into his trunk. Rick left to return the car at the San Diego airport and planned to meet me at the bus station. Xavier and I headed for *Aduana* and the obligatory paperwork shuffle with Customs.

On the boat, I was in charge of keeping our immigration and port check-in papers in order. Upon arrival at each office for check in, I routinely gave the forms to Rick and walked a few paces behind. Men did business with men. I knew that and now I was even more grateful for Xavier's help.

A starched and uniformed official sat at his 1940s desk. The surface was smooth and only my paperwork sat in the middle. He stood and left the room for long minutes, returning with another, equally starched man with a badge. They examined each page of the forms and their carbon copies. The men conferred and left again.

I was impatient and trying to hide it. Xavier motioned for me to sit quietly, but not being in control was making me jumpy. I knew from the experiences of boating friends that it was possible that this could take more hours than I had. Another strong possibility was that I'd be charged more than the boat parts cost.

With Xavier's help, I answered questions about where I was going, where we'd been, where my husband was and why I needed these things in Mexico. I replied using my most respectful smile, simple English and no Spanish. I'd been in Mexico long enough to know that loud, bossy and rushed was not the way to get things done.

A metal chair scraped across the floor to my right. A door closed. The long red second hand on the wall ticked the time away. After nearly an hour, the first man picked up my papers and carried them to the desk where another man sat at a typewriter. Four identical uniforms stood by while the fifth painstakingly squared the corners of the new forms with old carbon paper. He hand rolled the papers into alignment. I couldn't take my eyes off the slow motion drama. I jumped at the first staccato bang of the keys.

When Xavier and I had a sheaf of typed forms and carbon copies, all stamped with an authoritative "whomp, whomp," I paid a small surcharge for the extra luggage. It seemed reasonable after so much negotiation. With Xavier's help I set up camp with my stack of ten bundles and boxes in front of the door where our bus would load.

I hugged him goodbye and sat down on a duffle bag. It made a comfortable chair, with a box as a back rest, and I leaned back to wait for Rick, surveying the waiting area.

Two men in coats and ties came from opposite directions and said hello with a handshake and a kiss on each cheek. How un-American, I thought. A young mother carried twins in a striped serape. The bold reds and blues illuminated the dark skin and chocolate eyes of the little ones. A woman sold tamales from a basket on her head. An American-looking couple in their 60s wore backpacks and canvas boating hats. They smiled and waved. I didn't know them but we looked like people who might know each other.

I looked at my watch. Where was Rick? A couple of hours ago I was priding myself on being a relaxed and seasoned traveler. Now I was freaking out. In twelve minutes the bus would leave without us. My breathing was coming in short bursts. I was the child who couldn't find her parents at the fair. I paced in tight circles. "Stop chewing your cuticles. Breathe. If you miss this bus you'll take the next one," I counseled myself.

With six minutes to spare, I saw Rick through the crowd, about fifty yards away. I raised my arms to wave and he gave me the iguana nod while he jogged toward me. I couldn't help but laugh.

"Hey, want some help with that stuff lady?" he asked as he approached, slinging the duffle bags over his shoulders in a smooth motion.

"Oh my God, I was so worried. What took you so long?" I bleated, hoisting the golf bag straps onto my shoulders. We shoved and carried the mountain of gear through the gates just as the driver was closing the luggage compartment.

The air conditioning inside the bus was cool. I lay my head on the crisply ironed white headrest cover and watched the images on the movie screen hanging in front of me. We opened the bag of sandwiches and soda we'd been given when we boarded. "Very civilized way to travel," Rick said and I agreed.

The movies were in English and more violent than I liked but I was mesmerized by the Spanish subtitles and skimmed for words I recognized. An actor on screen said "You shot him in the head." I heard, "*tu*" and "*cabeza.*" "You" and "head." It wasn't the same as being fluent but I felt relatively wise. And relaxed.

The twenty-two–hour bus ride was punctuated by the appearance of vendors at every stop. Some pushed whatever they were selling through the windows and others got on the bus. Their wicker baskets were piled with tantalizing homemade tamales and burritos. Children offered Chiclets, oranges and soft drinks in plastic bags with a straw. It was a carnival and we had seats.

It seemed that every four to six hours we got a new driver and Rick wondered where they came from, marveling that they were always on time. At one stop, Rick pointed out a trap door just behind the passenger side front wheel. At the next fuel stop we saw the relief driver crawling out of the drawer where he apparently slept between shifts. That explained the miracle of the on-time replacement drivers.

After about twelve hours on the bus, we came to an unexpected stop and parked on the side of the narrow highway with an even skinnier shoulder. The driver made an announcement, but the only words I understood were *equipaje* (luggage), *caminar* (to walk) and *cambio* (change). Not knowing what was going on and with no one to ask, we followed our travel mates off the bus. We were alarmed but no one else seemed to be. A Mexican businessman, fluent in English, saw our confusion and explained.

"There's a bus strike that keeps this bus from continuing. We're at the buffer zone between the two factions. See the northbound bus over there with its lights on?"

We nodded like dolls with springs for necks.

"We board that bus to continue south," he explained. "And the passengers on that bus will go north on this bus. It's the Mexican solution," he said, pointing to the bus in front of us making a "U" turn.

We thanked him. With a bemused look, Rick said, "Hey, whatever it takes. Let's get crackin'. We've got a lot to move." It took us two trips to get all our boxes and bags transferred and we were the last to finish. Our fellow passengers applauded when we took our seats.

Rumbling south, we talked quietly, agreeing that we liked what had been called "The Mexican solution" better than the one Americans might have come up with. We would probably be stuck back at the border and the buses wouldn't be running at all.

At 9:00 AM, approaching a Pemex gas station, I was startled to see boating friends jog by. We hopped off and I hollered, sprinting toward them, waving both hands over my head. "Carol, Curly, *PNY*." They were from New York so their boat was *Princess New York*. We did a four-person bear hug in the street. They were out for a morning run and *PNY* was moored at a nearby anchorage. We had no time to chat. Our bus was leaving.

Cruising was like that. One friend described our relationships as "sandlot friends." We met like children in a park who play with whoever is there and become great pals even though they'll most likely never meet again. We had lots of those kinds of friends in the cruising community.

In *La Paz*, we settled back into our cruising life, remembering that friends could be for an hour or a lifetime. I had always struggled with loss when friends moved on and lost touch. Throughout my life, I'd made new friends but despaired when one went astray. Sailing was teaching me that there are friends for a season, friends for a reason and friends for a lifetime. They are all valuable and serve different purposes in our lives. Making new friends was part of what we loved about the cruising lifestyle and a good reason to continue.

Time and troubles had doused the image of *Nanook* crossing an ocean and we reined in the scope of our plans. We rationalized that still being in Mexico and not in the South Pacific was an extended shakedown cruise since we'd been so inexperienced when we started. Again, we re-shaped our itinerary, thinking that it would be fun to spend the summer in the Sea of Cortez, sail south with the fleet in the fall and transit the Panama Canal, exploring the Caribbean. It sounded exciting enough.

But that required a dependable engine. Being list makers, we surveyed the engine parts strewn around the cockpit and pulled out a trusty legal pad and pen. Rick enumerated our options and I organized them on paper.

1. Hire another mechanic on the theory that someone new might finally find what was wrong.
2. Put in a new engine. Questions – how would we pay for it and how would we get it into Mexico and installed?
3. Bundle the parts in a duffle bag and Rick would go to Mazatlan where he'd get repairs done.

We chose door number three.

The breezes were balmy and we had time to sort it all out. I determined that troubles in Mexico, where we had friends and the time to enjoy them, was a better life than returning to home ownership and jobs. So far.

We sailed for another few weeks until, with *Nanook* and me snug in a marina, Rick hauled the heavy bag of parts onto our folding dock cart and set off in search of a solution. The work we'd been advised would be available in *Mazatlan* wasn't and he ended up back in San Diego. With Rick off the boat I spread my projects out, not needing to be considerate or to share the space. I walked the length of the boat without a *con permiso* and re-organized storage bins without a compromise. I ate when I felt like it. Without Rick, life was uncomplicated but it lacked energy and fun. I missed him.

I wrote in my journal.

> Reality is the marina but I gaze out to sea and listen to the surf. Traveling on the pliable water, under the sky and untethered is a memory and a

dream. For now, my life is tranquil with unlimited Mexican sunshine, fresh fish and free time.
It's a lovely description of "trouble."

I crewed a boat from the anchorage into a slip in the marina. I sold a few items of clothing to a *tienda* owner, picked up faxes in town for one boater and groceries for another. It was a 1940s lifestyle of neighborly assistance. I spent my afternoons at the swimming pool and two mornings a week in a writers critique group. I played Scrabble in the evenings and I looked forward to Rick's return.

I won a spa gift certificate in a regatta raffle drawing. Wrapped in a plush, sea green towel, I inhaled the heady sweet smell of roses. Soft fingers rubbed lotion into my neck and massaged my jaw muscles. Uunder the spell of aromatherapy, I questioned my choice of life as a vagabond, denied these luxuries.

The spa treatment took my thoughts back to our previous life – the one we had left on purpose. The one with creature comforts.

I tiptoed on freshly pedicured feet from one fragrant room to the next. From roses to fields of lavender and then to an oatmeal body scrub, on to a lemon oil massage and a steaming soak surrounded by candles.

The attendant walked me down a hall and eased me onto a massage table. There, utterly naked, while soft hands massaged my lower spine and hips, I floated in and out of sleep. My mind took flight and images of myself at sixty, eighty and if I was lucky, far beyond into very, very old age appeared.

With my eyes closed, I saw a woman who looked more like my mother than me, but this woman wasn't dressed in my mother's country club outfit with sparkly shoes. She wore rubber-soled shoes and a smile. She drank box wine from a glass with a pencil-thin stem and cradled a scrapbook of memories in her lap.

From her rocking chair, she gazed out the window, over roof tops and across a parking lot. But what she saw was a boat with billowing sails. The image changed to snow falling softly on parallel ski tracks. Like a computer-generated slide show from her travels, one image faded into the next. A motorcycle rounded a curve on a steep mountain road; a small woman, fully clad in leather under a full face mask helmet rode on the back. Castles. Waterfalls. Sunrises. Seashells. Picnics. Birds in flight. A sunflower. A grandchild. A house with a red door and a porch swing.

Strong hands worked the muscles of my thighs. Jimmy Buffett had said something in his book about fifty being not just another birthday but "a reluctant milepost on the way to wherever we're supposed to wind up." I liked that idea. When the massage ended, I rolled over, wishing there were CliffsNotes for the book of life.

I sipped tea, wrapped in my Turkish robe. I had loved being coddled, powdered and massaged. I enjoyed luxuries, but I was content without them, too. Gazing through the steam at my freshly polished toes, I counted my blessings.

It was winter and I had a tan. I wiggled the big toe on my right foot, one.

The girls are focused and seem to be happy. I wiggled the next two toes. AJ was starting her career in Chicago. Lisa was a senior and would graduate in May with a teaching credential.

My parents were healthy. I waggled the last two toes on my right foot.

I had sold an article to a sailing magazine. That's number six, I thought, wiggling the big toe on my left foot.

I was learning to speak Spanish. Seven.

and I was content. Eight.

With two left over for the future.

I inhaled deeply, holding my face over the steam from my sweet tea. An emerging me was out in the open and I didn't see how I could stuff her into the old packaging, like the sponge Christmas card we got every year when I was a kid. My brother and I took turns pressing it into a bowl of water. We watched the letters emerge until it read "Merry Christmas from the Hambys" in four-inch letters. My life was that sponge and it couldn't possibly return to its old self, I thought, putting the tea cup down.

When Rick returned to *Nanook*, a diesel mechanic in the fleet reassembled the motor and gave it a test run. It looked as if our problems were solved, so we celebrated by topping off the diesel and water tanks, stocking fresh food and ice and paying the marina bill.

After forty-seven days in the marina, leaving felt like that first departure from our home port in Long Beach. We were full of energy and nervous anticipation. Just outside the harbor we set the sails and cut the engine. As the sun rose in the sky, the winds increased and the seas steepened. The ocean bucked and we tumbled down the front of one wave and into the next. The smooth tiller lay in my hand, responding easily to my touch. The sails were full. The rigging buzzed. I threw my head back and hollered, "Yippee, ride 'em cowpoke." I was a cowgirl in my first rodeo.

Rick looked up from the book he was reading. "Sounds like you're having fun."

"I guess I am," I nodded and slapped my hip with my free hand as if it were a bridle on the horse's flank.

About three hours later, the wind died and I fired up the rebuilt engine. It purred and we held a steady course.

"Honey, you'll never believe this," I said.

"What?"

"The temperature and pressure gauges are perfect. We should take a photo and tape it over the real gauges." I was sick of the needle being in the red but he just shook his head in reply.

Late that evening Rick called for me to join him in the cockpit. The seas were sloppy, but the diesel was chugging through the jumbled waves.

"Honey, the instructions were to shut 'er down at ten hours and change the oil."

Rick could win a medal in an Olympic Oil Change event if they ever scheduled one. I reluctantly took the tiller and turned off the motor. Without power we tossed like clothes in a washing machine.

This time wasn't an award winning performance. Hot oil burned Rick's crotch and leg. He dropped the dip stick into the bilge. He swore long and loud in new combinations of words and used the BBQ tongs to retrieve the dip stick. Thirty minutes later, Rick sat with a bag of ice on his burns and we were underway again.

We were cautiously optimistic but it was short lived. The diesel overheated within the next hour and we weren't charging the batteries either.

All the time and money we'd invested were a big zero. Rick raised the sails despite the lack of wind. It would be a long night.

> "It was the sailboats with their gleaming white sails set against the blue sky that spoke to my wanderlust."
>
> JOHN HIGHAM,
> *360 DEGREES LONGITUDE*

CHAPTER 17

Sea of Dreams

LEAVING *MAZATLAN*, WE slid across water smooth as polished onyx. My internal rhythm matched our movement the way my heartbeat echoed my pulse and our little cow swung like a metronome. There was no moon to light our path. The radio, too, was quiet since no cruising friends were making this passage with us.

I was on watch, reading a tattered copy of *The Perfect Storm* I'd picked up at a book swap. It was a poor choice of reading material on the ocean but the sea was calm. I went below to check the radar. When I returned to the cockpit, a sliver of moon had found a hole in the clouds and light danced on the water like headlights from a parked car.

I gasped.

An open fishing boat was less than two hundred yards behind us. I could see four fishing poles and two dark shapes covered in blankets, probably sleeping fishermen. I put both hands over my mouth, stifling the scream that threatened.

The light was temporary. Clouds pulled a blanket across the moon, drawing a darkness so complete it was like being invisible. My heart raced and I peered into the night wondering if other fishing boats were in our path.

When dawn broke, we anchored in Turquoise Bay, a secluded hole near *La Paz*. We'd been underway, sharing the on-watch duty for forty-eight hours and had traveled 230 miles.

After a breakfast of pork chops, applesauce, a mushroom and garlic omelet and orange juice, we dropped the dinghy into the cobalt water and went to shore. Walking carefully between the thorny cactus plants and scrub brush, we explored the desert.

Vibrant spots of color burst from the buds of cactus, acacia bloomed and the yellow sand changed before our eyes to rust or gold depending on the angle of the sun. I began to have fantasies of becoming a painter. "Whoa, girl. You're in the middle of a few new lives already," I thought.

Swarms of black and tiny bugs drove us out of what had been an idyllic anchorage. They buzzed our noses, eyelids and ears. Where clouds of the little buggers landed it looked like we'd dumped out ashes from a fireplace. They were persistent and in early afternoon we surrendered and broke camp.

Entering *La Paz* is like playing connect the dots with

channel markers. A long-fingered sand bar makes a direct approach impossible. We zigged and zagged, carefully reading the depth finder and charts.

While I enjoyed the solitude of being underway, now I was giddy for an ice cream cone. Once we were checked in at the marina office, Rick and I agreed that boat projects could wait and we would go in search of ice cream. First we rinsed a week's worth of salt water from our sticky bodies using a hose on the dock. Towel drying, Rick put on a clean T-shirt, dry swim trunks and flip-flops. I ran my fingers through my short hair, tossed a sleeveless dress over my head and slipped into red flip-flops. We were clean and dry, which was as dressed up as we got. Hand in hand, we walked to town.

In the weeks that we called *La Paz* home, we abandoned *Nanook*'s galley and ate from the street carts. Bacon-wrapped hot dogs were decadent as well as addictive in a bakery fresh bun. My favorite crispy fish tacos were filled with fried oysters and drizzled in vinegar. Late at night, soft baked potatoes wrapped in foil were ready to be loaded with cheeses, cream sauces, diced vegetables and shredded meats. Fruit chunks on skewers always tasted good and we licked the juices that ran down our fingers.

While all the cart food was worthy, the vendor masterpiece was a *coctel de camarones*. These shrimp cocktails weren't even distant cousins to the cuticle-size, swimming in lemony ketchup kind they served to the north. Here, the shrimp were the size of a fist and drowning in lime juice, chopped tomatoes and fresh cilantro. Instead of a fork, we lifted them with corn tortilla shovels hot off the grill. and, of course, we always found an ice cream cone to finish the meal.

Wandering the shops, I bought hand-embroidered pillows for the settee. Store windows displaying leather chairs and painted tables tantalized me with visions of furnishing a house again. My yearning to build a nest caught me off-guard and flew in direct conflict with the curious, wandering person I had become.

"If home is where my stuff is," I reminded myself, "I need to be satisfied with what I've got." Sighing out loud, I left the store, giving just one last gaze over my shoulder at the four-foot mirror framed in hand-painted ceramic tiles. It was expensive. It was big and breakable. I lived on a boat and on a budget. But I wanted it and the tug stayed.

Lisa flew to Mexico on her spring break. We went on an all-girl sail. We snorkeled and had long talks. I was reminded that today's crisis often floats away if you give it space.

After nearly a month in *Marina La Paz*, we reluctantly set a date for departure. I asked out loud, to no one in particular, "Do you need to move your boat to call yourself a cruiser?" If we spent more than a few months in one place, I thought it made us expatriate live-aboards, not cruisers. Despite the obvious expectation that a boat should leave the harbor, every marina we saw had its share of permanent residents. It was an inexpensive way to live a good life but we hadn't been tempted to commit to a single location.

We anchored in the bay near the marina, waiting for a package of mail to arrive. One morning about 5:00 AM we were sound asleep in the V-berth when a voice calling "Skipper, Skipper" at the volume of a stage whisper came from somewhere near our bow. We crawled out of bed and padded into the cockpit.

A thirty-something man was waving from the helm of his twenty-five–foot sailboat about thirty feet away. He said, "Help me, I'm floating ashore." Our first reaction was to wonder why he didn't just drop a bow or stern anchor, start the engine or raft his dinghy to the side of the boat. This man was in distress but wasn't taking any of those actions, so Rick pulled on clothes that I tossed at him in haste.

We launched the dinghy and Rick roared off. Apparently the guy's very lightweight anchor had very little chain, mostly rope, and had been pulled loose by the wake of a passing fishing boat. Now the line was wrapped around his prop. Rick solved his problem and the unprepared fellow fled to the marina.

Our mail packet came so we said goodbye to *La Paz* and sailed north into the Sea of Cortez. We motor sailed below the red-tinged cliffs, streaked with horizontal lines of yellow and gray and I read and re-read my Mother's Day cards from AJ and Lisa. Both said that they were proud of me. I respected their opinions and glowed in the praise.

Sculpted sandstone cliffs hung on the horizon. We were alone except for the shrimpers we passed, the fifty- to sixty-foot boats with poles extended wide, dragging their nets. The shrimpers' chatter kept the VHF radio crackling, and trying to decipher what they were saying kept me engaged.

The Baja is a brutally beautiful land. From the air, it probably looks like a long stretch of empty water, but up close, rays leapt, dolphins played and whales spouted. The shoreline, too, looked barren from a distance but on foot we found signs of life. We heard bugs chewing on plants, watched the circling vultures, *los zopilotes*, and followed the trails and tracks of critters that roamed at night.

Walking in the sand was like steppng on a stove top. Being too hot for tourist season, the campgrounds were empty but since our boat insurance required us to stay in protected marinas or north of *La Paz* between June and October, we hung out in the Sea.

Every afternoon, we snorkeled to cool off. Neon fish swam between the rocks. Tube worms waved their feather duster tentacles. Opened anenomes looked like pink palm trees and shrimp with shiny gold eyes skittered among the rocks. I snorkeled for clams while Rick went deeper in search of scallops and lobster.

We crawled into our scuba gear at least once a week to explore deeper water. I struggled into the straps that held my scuba tank, secured the weight belt and squirmed to adjust the tight-fitting mask over my eyes and nose. I could hear my butterflies screaming. I counseled myself,

"Pay attention. Exhale slowly. Don't breathe through your nose."

Jumping into the water with a weight belt on still seemed counterintuitive. When I took swimming lessons as a child, the objective was to stay on top of the water. Now, here I was, miles from shore and in deep water wearing ten pounds of weight around my waist. I cleared my sinuses as I'd learned in class and descended to thirty feet, giving Rick a tentative thumbs-up "all's well" sign.

I wished that being underwater didn't make me a nervous nelly because paddling around in the middle of a Jacques Cousteau mural was astonishing. I swam through crowds of blue-and-yellow-striped fish the size of my hands. Four large turtles moved by on my left. Gliding, I moved through a mass of angel and butterfly fish with puffers and porgies below me. Groupers with eyes circled in neon red made me want to laugh but I'd learned the hard way that laughing while snorkeling or scuba diving is a terrible idea.

Rick motioned for me to join him and I descended. A yellow moray eel wiggled by. Rick tugged at a giant scallop, broke it loose and dropped the six-inch shell into the mesh collection bag tied to his waist. He gave me a thumbs-up with a pantomime of eating it for lunch. Holding hands, we cruised the rocky crevices of the reefs.

Every few days we moved gradually north, anchoring in fat-fingered inlets between cliffs to hide from the summer winds. The powerful *chubascos* cleared the decks of everything we hadn't lashed down. I've never lived where tornados and cyclones rearrange the neighborhood but I guessed that a *chubasco* is similar.

Our first experience with the wind demon exploded without warning. Our dinghy was trailing peacefully behind Nanook and we were anchored in a calm cove when the wind arrived like a torpedo across the water. Suddenly, whitecaps turned into writhing foam, screaming and screeching. I felt like Dorothy in *The Wizard of Oz* except that I didn't have Auntie Em's storm cellar to hide in. My stomach did rolling somersaults while I grabbed towels and cushions before they turned into kites. Rick caught empty diesel and water jugs in flight. We looked like outfielders catching debris from an out-of-control ball machine.

While we were catching small items flying through the air, our dinghy took flight on her tether. Twirling in the wild wind, she flipped over. Upside down, she dove under the self-steering vane on the stern, puncturing the port pontoon. The wind had its way and slashed a six-foot tear before we could save it. Rick snapped a bridle to the bucking bow and cranked while I arm wrestled it like a three-hundred-pound slippery corpse. We hauled it onboard and lashed it to the stanchions.

The wind only lasted about twenty minutes. Our anemometer had clocked the *chubasco* at fifty to sixty knots. In the quiet that followed the storm, we surveyed the damage and with binoculars, Rick found our dinghy seat and oars on the beach. The seas were calm and paradise returned to its scorching self.

It took three weeks to get the dinghy repaired. Without it, we had no transportation off *Nanook* but we hitched a ride or borrowed a dinghy from friends until we were independent again.

Sailing into the anchorage in front of the village of *Nopolo*, we dropped the anchor. Our arrival unleashed an exodus. At least a dozen *pangas* motored out to see us. One wanted aspirin for a toothache. Most wanted fresh water in jugs they eagerly handed over our rail. All were curious. When language failed us, smiles and gestures communicated.

The air was silky and bearable at dawn but by midday it seared my skull. I slept in the cockpit, hoping to catch even the hint of a cooling breeze. Long before daybreak I heard voices. All I could see was a cluster of boats with their lights on. At sunrise, the fishermen pulled their loaded *panga*s onto the beach. Rick put on swim trunks and swam to shore to see what they had caught.

The men had been fishing for calamari; now they were cleaning the catch on the beach and tossing the two-by-three-foot squares of white flesh into their open boats. Rick stood alongside and worked with them, no words were needed or spoken. When they finished, the sun was high. The loaded *panga*s went back out to sea, motoring out of sight.

I watched the fishermen move across the sand to

their families for a meal and a siesta. Rick swam back to *Nanook*.

Over lunch Rick and I talked about the journey that the calamari would take: filleted in the hot sun, then transferred to the back of a pickup truck before being refrigerated about four hours later in a *Cabo San Lucas* restaurant. It would be punched into circles and served as "fresh sea scallops."

The next day I was stricken with a bout of spring cleaning. I pulled every single item from *Nanook*'s lockers and cupboards. Spare parts, a three-year-old zip-locked baggie of flour, a dented can of chili and two mystery cans that had lost their labels. Rick tossed a broken snorkel and a fin without its mate onto the growing pile. I didn't need an egg beater, a rusted flashlight, books we'd already read or a deck of cards with a missing three of diamonds. With the dinghy loaded, we went to shore and gave everything away. We walked up the street to the school and gave them a ream of copy paper and a bag of pens.

Sailing north out of *Nopolo*, we followed the aqua ribbon of water, rippling in the midday sun. My skin was a baked potato and I kept a fresh water spray bottle within reach all afternoon. We sailed between pale pink mountains on our left and dark purple on the right, with the sky blasting an intense blue. On approach to the village of *Agua Verde*, a cluster of thatched roofs emerged, lining the sandy beach. A dozen boats were anchored in the bay. I searched for words to describe it and again wished I was a painter.

When we were sure the anchor was holding, I dove into the water for a much-needed bath. Back on board, I wrote in my journal.

> A bath in the sea is luxurious. Rolling waves lift me for a view of the beach and set me gently back in my private trough. Soap bubbles refract into little rainbows and I'm a child again.

We'd only been there a few hours when a *panga* arrived, inviting us to a fiesta the next day. Cruisers love a party and we all launched our dinghies on cue, carrying plastic plates, silverware and drinks. We followed the dusty web of streets according to the hand-drawn map Ernesto had given us.

The party zone was Ernesto's fenced dirt yard. He had moved his children's cots outside the fence and set up tables. We feasted on stuffed clams, lobster, ceviche, white fish stew, beans, rice and tortillas.

The next morning, we returned to the village to explore. We walked by the school and gave each of the nine students a packet of gifts that included crayons, tablets of paper and toothbrushes. Sabrique and Justina giggled and hugged us, recognizing us from the party at their house the night before. We walked on, poking our heads into a darkened church.

Pigs rolled in a water hole under a tree. Fences around

the houses kept the pigs and goats out so that vegetables had a chance to grow in the hard-packed earth. A spider web of hoses delivered water in a snaking labyrinth of connections.

One house was the local *tienda*. I bought tired avocados, wrinkled tomatoes, two bruised onions and a jar of strawberry jam with a dented lid. I asked if they had any meats and the young boy told me to come back and they would have something for me. We left with my purchases in a string bag, wondering what we might get when we returned.

Cracked plaster houses in rows of faded sherbet all had unadorned dirt yards but the dust had been raked to Japanese garden perfection. Plastic bits clung to the leeward side of every tree and bush. It was obvious that there wasn't any trash pick-up service and the pigs wandered with such confidence that we decided they must belong equally to everyone.

We walked on and waved at familiar faces from the party. Clotheslines sagged between trees, a visual reminder that these towns had no electricity. In a stab at modern conveniences, solar panels jutted from roof tops and twisted wire-and-beer-can sculptures grew next to them, creating makeshift television antennas.

We returned to the *tienda* to pick up dinner. A warm bundle of burlap was placed in my arms with such tenderness that I wondered if it was alive. It was a chicken. Dead, cleaned and plucked.

Back on *Nanook*, I rubbed the chicken with lemon

and sprinkled it with garlic before putting it in the oven. While it baked, Rick and I snuggled on the bow sharing a cup of tequila and watching the stars click on. We were still saving electicity so the CD player was off and we listend to the music of a gentle surf kiss the shore.

In the morning we took the dinghy across the bay to a cruiser shrine. It's a legendary junkyard of art creations labeled with boat names, a testimony to the decades of cruisers who passed through. Arrangements varied from painted sea shells to carved rocks and bottles, used boat parts, hats, shoes, burgees and anchors. An ophthalmologist sailor we knew hung a mobile made from eyeglass lenses. We hung a less creative gift, a small, faded Mexican flag with *Nanook* written in felt-tip pen.

We walked alone on the beach, looking out at the boats. A cluster of cruisers tread water, resting on their styrofoam noodles. All that was visible were their bobbing canvas hats and they looked like a dozen corks set between the fluorescent ends of their floating tubes. It was a funny life but we loved it.

When we still owned a home and had jobs, Rick had read advice on what kind of boat to buy. The author had said that it was a very individual choice but she thought it was important to be able to say, at least, "Mine is the pretty one over there." *Nanook*'s off-white hull and soft canoe stern looked lovely lined up in the cruising fleet. Her charm was part of the romance of our sailing adventure, despite the white smoke that continued to billow from our exhaust.

When the engine wasn't overheating or smoking and the wind wasn't too strong and the seas not too tall, it was a great life. I filled my pockets with seashells and thought about where I would put them someday. I didn't know what part of the country we'd settle in. It might be a loft in a city or a cabin in the mountains and I knew that I didn't need to know. For a veteran planner, this was progress.

We stayed in some anchorages for a few weeks, others for just a few hours. Getting underway involved a drill: check the oil, hoist the dinghy, secure the outboard. Close the port holes, bungee everything that moved and make an entry in the log. While Rick hand-cranked the anchor off the bottom, I lay across the V-berth bunks, stacking the anchor chain to avoid tangles in the locker.

Everywhere we went, we were approached by fishermen in *pangas* who brought goodies to us. In one anchorage, Manuel introduced himself and offered twelve giant sea scallops and a lobster along with an ice chest full of shaved ice. Rick gave him a T-shirt and a bottle of rum in exchange. At *Modesto*, Enrique had given us four lobsters in exchange for four beers. His young daughter was with him and I gave her a yellow hair bow on a clip and a red pen. Gabriel brought ice, a triggerfish and a parrot fish. It seemed it would be impossible to starve.

Nearly every night, the sun danced and flashed, bathing the horizon in gold and setting the shore on fire. It bled into the sea and stained the sky. Darkened silhouettes of saguaro cactus grew long with the sinking sun and stood like sentinels at the base of the low mountains.

But one morning our friends on *Steppin' Out* hailed us on the VHF radio.

"*Nanook, Nanook*, this is *Steppin' Out*."

"*Hola*, we're here, what's up?" I answered.

"Hey Christie, there was emergency traffic for you guys on the Ham net this morning. A phone patch from Colorado is trying to reach you."

My siesta lifestyle evaporated and tension gripped my neck.

"Oh my God, did they say anything else?"

"Sorry, no details. Just that if anyone knew where you were to have you tune to the *Manana Net*.

We did and learned that Rick's mother was in a coma. We headed for *Puerto Escondido* where there was an airport and a phone. We were powerless to hurry but our thoughts raced. Flo hadn't been well and there was nothing we could have done for her even if we'd still had a house and jobs. But now Rick felt guilty. Two days later Rick went to shore and used a phone. His sister said simply, "Mom died."

Back on board I was at the helm and Rick sat on the bow, meditating. He thought about flying to Colorado and decided against it. All I could do was give him the space to think. It was odd to feel so separate; we'd been living a box-step life, nearly always within an arm's reach of each other. Now, I could be supportive and caring but I was really apart, not a part.

After a few hours we sailed into a cluster of rays. With their ten- to twelve-foot wingspans, they looked like batman boats with aerodynamic bodies and electric blue eyes. Rick stood and pointed, distratcted from his thoughts by the creatures lifting and diving out of our path. He turned to look at me, sending me the iguana raised-chin signal. And I knew he'd be all right given some time to absorb his loss.

From the anchorage at *Santispac* the nearest markets were in *Mulege*, which was too far to walk so we stood beside the road with our thumbs out. American license plates roared by but the first Mexican truck braked in a flurry of dust. We scrambled over the rusty tailgate and wedged ourselves between cases of Pepsi and a dozen crates that smelled like fish.

We sped past three little boys lugging buckets of water almost as big as they were. A woman wearing a floral print dress walked with a basket on her head and a girl with pigtails tugged an enormous pig on a rope. We passed a woman moving a broom, two men riding burros, a boy peeling an orange,and ragged wash on clotheslines.

When the truck slowed, our driver slapped his hand on the door. We knew from experience that meant the ride was over. We clambered out and the truck sputtered, shifted gears and disappeared around a curve leaving a scarf of dust in its wake. We turned right and walked the rest of the way to town. Three chickens strutted by, pecking at the dusty red powder road.

On the main street a sign read:
Oasis de paz,
Ambiente de reposo,
Que al cuerpo de solaz,
Y al alma gozo.
I copied it and got the translation later. It said, "Oasis of peace. Environment of repose that gives solace to the body and pleasure to the soul." I believed it.

Back onboard, *Nanook* rolled in the hot bay and Rick straddled the engine as if it were a hobby horse. Neither the solar panels nor the engine batteries were holding a charge. I wrote in my journal.

> But a lovely swim and the stars last night balance the difficulties.

A *panga* approached, the shirtless fisherman waving something large and orange above his head. When he came alongside, I saw that it was a lobster about the size of a shoe box.

"*Quieres una regalo?*" he asked.

We happily accepted his gift. It wouldn't fit in my soup pot but I sliced, boiled and barbecued the enormous slipper lobster. When I shared the story with a cruiser in the next anchorage, she said. "Oh, they tried to give us something, but we were afraid." So sad; knowing a little of the language was important.

That afternoon I was on watch and Rick sat on the

PLOTTING A NEW COURSE

bow with a book. I tipped my chin skyward and inhaled the salty breeze. The ocean lapped at the hull and the wind whispered in the rigging.

I looked around and thought, the only thing out here that isn't blue is *Nanook*. I thought of other blues I liked. Blueberries, blue eyes, blue jeans, blue footed boobie blue, Smurf blue, blues music, delft china blue, blue pansies. My world was an ink bottle. and every blue had a different tone, a unique taste or smell. I watched the shades of blue go by, wondering how the word "blue" ever got associated with sadness. I vowed that if I ever again said, "I'm feeling blue," it would be a good thing.

When the sun dropped that night, the sea bubbled with the energy of birds performing touch and go maneuvers. "Who needs television?" I thought.

At 10:00 PM the black sky was a mass of yellow and white dots, phosphorescence caused by jellyfish popping in bursts of golden champagne in the dark water. I stood naked on the deck in a mild warm breeze, at peace and in awe.

> *"Once you have traveled, the voyage never ends, but is played out over and over again in the quietest chambers. The mind can never break off from the journey."*
>
> PAT CONROY

CHAPTER 18
Off the Boat

WITH LAND-BASED HEARTS Rick and I left *Nanook* more often than most cruisers. When we were at anchor we took day-trips and when a marina was an option, we traveled further inland.

A bus took us to *Cuernavaca* for a language immersion program where we lived for two weeks with a Mexican family. We hiked in the Copper Canyon, arriving by train from *Mazatlan*. On that adventure we met a cluster of partying Australians. Late into the night we drank dark rum, played cards, laughed until the sun came up and promised to stay in touch. Which we didn't, because travel friends seldom do.

We spent a night in the silver mining town of *Taxco* and the villages of *Tlaqepaque*, *Guanajuato* and *San Miguel Allende*. A bus took us to *Huatulco* and *Oaxaca*. We traveled by bus, train and car.

I kept wanting more.

DURING OUR THIRD winter in Mexico we bought a used car. A network of rural roads meanders through Mexico. Most were peppered with potholes, roaming animals and obstacles that included cars traveling in the wrong lane without headlights. We knew that it was customary to occupy the lane with the least potholes but we never found out why Mexicans liked to drive at night with their headlights off. But they did.

On one of our escapades, we rounded a curve to find a semi truck in our lane. It was carrying a load of tomatoes, going fast. It lunged, leaning heavily to the left. Tomatoes flew through the air. Smoke rose from the tires into Rick's open window. I screamed. Rick white-knuckled us onto the nonexistent shoulder, missed the truck and only splattered a few tomatoes.

"Jeez, that was close. We could have been ketchup," he said, smiling over his right shoulder at me.

I managed a tense laugh that sounded more like choking. I patted his hand on the gear shift. "I don't know how you missed him. Our angels must be on duty even on land," I said.

We drove past men riding horses and women scrubbing laundry on rocks. When a town appealed to us we parked and walked for a couple of hours. Sometimes we spent one night. Or two.

Pigs and chickens shared the streets with as much propriety as pedestrians and none showed any sense of urgency. We shared the road with bicycles, too, and they weren't the weekend exercise kind. This was serious transportation on old balloon tire bikes. It was common to see a man and his bicycle jettison into the bushes to avoid oncoming traffic. With the reflexes of a good racquetball player, Rick played Mexican dodge ball on the roadways and it didn't seem to faze anyone except me.

Speed bumps were a practical solution for slowing traffic. A *tope* sign indicated a single bump and a *vibrador* meant lots of little ones were coming up. They effectively reduced speeds and had the added benefit of helping the young roadside entrepreneurs. When we slowed for the bumps, ardent salesmen shoved their wares through our car windows. Bottles of Coca Cola. Bags of dried pineapple and shaved coconut. Gold chains with dangling crosses. Whenever we slowed down we were offered something for sale or someone with a rag and a bottle of Windex climbed on the hood to wash the windshield. It was like being swarmed by bees, but I preferred it to Americans asking for spare change with no exchange of services.

During one drive out of the mountains, yellow butterflies splattered the windshield like mustard on a stadium hot dog. I asked Rick if he could even see through the mess.

"Not really," he said. "But it'll get washed when we slow down, no doubt about it."

Road construction slowed us down, too. A row of

small rocks in the road diverted traffic into one lane, merging with cars going the opposite direction. This meant "road construction ahead" if you'd driven enough miles to recognize the signs. No earth movers, dump trucks, flares or orange cones. The construction crew was always a couple of skinny men with wheelbarrows and shovels.

When possible, we opted for the *rutas cuotas,* toll roads, for both safety and speed. Every hour or so we stopped to pay another toll. They were expensive but predictable. It was the stops for *frutas, vegetales o drogas* that got our attention. The guards looked like fourteen-year-olds with Uzis. We didn't have anything to hide but the stops always made us nervous. We spoke some Spanish but we mostly smiled, nodded and prayed our way through.

At one such stop, we were confronted by a mountain of hay bales. Behind the stacks, armed men crouched with their guns aimed. When guns give directions, it limits conversation. They motioned for us to park the car on planks over a hole in the ground, like a homemade version of a Jiffy Lube. Four men dropped into the hole while a half dozen of their *compadres* pointed guns at us. Even for chatty me it was easy to be quiet. The contents from nearby cars were piled on the pavement: ice chests, suitcases, pillows and infant seats. The men motioned us on without even opening our car doors. Why they emptied some cars and not others, we never found out.

On one drive, the continuous ridge of mountains

undulated like the spine of a dinosaur to the east. Rick slowed for burros laden with long stalks of something bushy on the ends, trudging in our lane. We paid twenty-three dollars for a room on the beach. It was scruffy but had a refrigerator and air conditioning that made noise but not much else. Rick went to the lobby to watch an NFL game and I sat on our patio listening to the ocean's music.

The next night we stayed in *Santiago Ixcuintla*, a Huichol community. We walked by a church where a funeral was in progress. It was almost Christmas and about 85 degrees. "Frosty the Snowman" blared from the loudspeakers in the town plaza. I was certain that we were the only two within a hundred miles who knew the lyrics of that song or could describe frost. I bought a cluster of plump purple grapes from a boy with a wheelbarrow full.

The Huichols wore colorful embroidered clothing and bright scarves. I tried to be unobtrusive, taking the photo of a man gloriously festooned in a flat hat trimmed with bobbing balls. I bought beaded Christmas ornaments for a future life when I would have a house and a big tree again. Huichol handicrafts included masks, beadwork and pictures made with colorful yarn laid intricately into beeswax. We loaded the trunk, wondering where we would put everything when we got back to *Nanook*.

We were headed for the village of *Mexcaltitán*, so we drove north on a narrow road that we shared with more

Mexcaltitán, Nay. México

bulls and pigs than cars. In less than an hour, the road ended abruptly. All that was in front of us was brown water, a liquid desert shimmering in the sun and just as quiet, until the sound of an outboard broke the silence. We stepped into a twenty-foot boat that could have belonged to Lewis and Clark except for the shirtless Mexican and the motor.

The island of *Mexcaltitán* has no cars and the streets are recessed two feet lower than the sidewalks. During rainy season they become canals, navigated by canoes propelled with poles. Now they were dry and dusty.

The island is an oval with streets running out like the spokes of a wheel, connecting with a circular street, called Venecia Circle, that runs all the way around the island. The town's two thousand residents are mostly descendants of just two families and the walls of the buildings were constructed with mud-coated mangrove stakes.

Legend says that the two-hundred-year pilgrimage of the Aztecs began here. They were in search of a sign – an eagle, perched on a prickly pear cactus, devouring a serpent. The image is the center of the Mexican flag.

We walked past shrimp drying on the walkways and watched a young girl lower a bucket through a trap door to pull out fresh water, *agua dulce*. After getting doused once, I kept a wary eye out for sudden movement because we'd seen buckets of water being tossed from windows and doors. It was an efficient way to keep the dust down and to dispose of mop water but it made using the sidewalks hazardous.

After a couple of hours, we stopped for a beer and hired another boat to take us back to the car. I asked the driver if he would give us a ride around the island instead of going straight to the landing. He responded, "*Si. Es mi regalo.*" I was glad I knew enough Spanish to accept his gift.

Most of our bus rides were quite comfortable. We'd enjoyed movies, sandwiches and air conditioning. The bus trip along the coast from *Acapulco* to the southern port town of *Huatulco* was an exception. We left at 8:00 PM and had only been underway about an hour when the bus rolled gently to a stop in the middle of what looked like nowhere. It didn't take long to realize the problem was mechanical. Our driver repaired the radiator with a section of hose he got from a passing bus using a machete and duct tape pulled from a passenger's suitcase. The fourth repair stop was at 6:00 in the morning. I didn't doze through any of the stops because I had the only flashlight on the bus and the driver politely returned it after each use.

Passengers stood in the aisles and didn't seem to mind. The total absence of visible irritability amazed me. My American brain wanted to arrive on schedule but all around me, my fellow passengers, all native Mexicans, appeared to be accepting the delays without a fuss. I mused that their lives probably hadn't changed for generations and maybe that gave them this incredible level of patience. Or, when you expect nothing are you satisfied when that's what you get? If they expected repaired buses would they get better buses or the same equipment accompanied by frustration? My Spanish wasn't good enough to discuss the idea so I was left with no answers.

When the bus stopped again, I got out to see if I could find a bathroom since the one on the bus had been out of order for the last few hours. I was greeted by rooster music on the cool morning air. Ducking under a clothes line, I asked a woman wielding a broom for permission. She was giving her dirt yard the tender care I had given to shiny hardwood floors. She nodded "yes" and I followed her.

We passed two rotund pigs, one scrawny goat and a dry patch of cornstalks before we got to a three-sided shack with a banana palm roof. The woman wiped both hands on the floral apron cinched around her ample waist as if to clean them before lifting a bucket that looked filthy to me. She demonstrated that when I was through I should pour the bucket of water down the hole. I nodded and smiled my thanks.

Back on the bus, I wondered what the woman with the broom, laundry line, and toilet expects from her life. Is it possible that she's essentially happier than her American counterpart? She looked happy to me. Do ice makers and food processors improve anything? I looked at the scenery we were passing. The nearest light bulb was probably a five-hour walk. I pulled out my journal.

> I came to see the inner workings of Mexican life and here they are. Vacationers who make hotel reservations from home, demand that English be spoken and require private bathrooms drive themselves away from the culture they say they want to experience. Traveling with a guide and a group, requiring air conditioning and ice cubes, keeps us from what we came to see. I think I'll call it Lazy Boy travel. The sights flow past without any participation from the traveler. He might as well have stayed home, watching television from his recliner.
>
> Our travels are intimate and I like that but I struggle with my inner American.

The bus stopped for every man, woman, chicken,

pig and child in a school uniform that flagged us down. All day and all night passengers climbed on and off the bus with their lumpy bundles. At one thirty-minute stop we bought cheese sandwiches and found a pay phone to call Lisa. I left a message on her answering machine. "Hi, Sweetie. I'm at a pay phone so I'll keep it short. Love you. Hope everything's going well. I'll call again in about a week."

After almost twenty-four hours on the bus, we arrived in *Huatulco*. The cobbled streets were clean and wide, anchored by a *zócalo* in the center with shops spreading out from there. Coffee smells mingled with sidewalk grills. The aroma of seared beef rose to my nostrils and after the stale bus air, I inhaled deeply.

We walked by shops peddling artwork and pretty clothes, *Oaxacan* cheeses and hundreds of kinds of mole sauces. If there were any T-shirt or trinket shops for tourists I happily didn't see them. I could have explored for hours but we needed to find a hotel. We settled on *Posada Michele*. It had a large bed, a small balcony, a ceiling fan and a private bathroom. There wouldn't be any running water for a few hours, or as it turned out, for the next two days, but the price was right.

We rented motor scooters and explored the area's nine bays and thirty-four beaches. We snorkeled and trekked through the jungle. Thirty yards from the water, with our toes in white sand, we drank *Micheladas*, a salt-rimmed beer mixed with tomato juice. While our lunch order of octopus and rice was being cooked, women selling seashells strung a necklace for me.

Back in our room, we were ready for a shower but the water wasn't running so I asked the front desk for a bucket. We hauled the over-flowing buckets to our room and showered by throwing the contents at each other. After four days we headed inland to see *Oaxaca*.

Rick raked coffee beans at a plantation. We explored the village of *Pochutla* and the narrow road grew steeper. We were climbing to 10,000 feet. Rivers of liquid chocolate streamed across the road where the highway had washed away. The bus forded the river bed and men laid rocks on the bank so we could climb back onto the highway.

Descending from the mountains we arrived in *Oaxaca*, a center of culture and art. My first glimpse was of pastel storefronts and narrow streets. Shiny dark-haired children in school uniforms walked beside their mothers.

We stayed in *Oaxaca* and visited the neighboring towns. In *Arrazola*, we watched teen-age boys carve the rare copal wood into *alebrijes*. Young girls painted the whimsical animal figures with rows of bright-colored dots. We negotiated for one that had been signed by all three Jimeniz brothers. The large carving was in the shape of a polar bear and we rationalized the expenditure by telling ourselves that it would always remind us of our *Nanook* years.

The weekly market at *Zaachila* wasn't for tourists. It was for the neighboring villagers, selling their goods to each other. Pigs rode in wheelbarrows. Men carted wood on their shoulders. They sold fruit, bamboo, rugs and nuts. Women carried turkeys over their arms like purses. I loved it.

We walked away from the market and into Cathedral *Santo Domino*. The altars were made of real gold. We watched black pottery being made and spent a day wandering the ruins of *Monte Alban*, a Zapotec city of 40,000 people in 500 BC. At *Mitla*, we stood at a meditation site for priests in 800 BC where the etchings on the walls are still visible. A tomb that held eight bodies almost three

thousand years ago had a rock carved in the shape of a pillow. I caressed it, thinking about change.

At a mescal processing plant we learned how the heart of the maguey cactus is harvested, roasted in a deep pit and covered with dirt before it's stripped into shavings and fermented. An ox turned the wheel that ran the mill, turning the sinewy cactus into a pungent liquor. In the pueblo, *Tlacolula*, we visited Gustavo and tasted the brew, a cousin of tequila.

Rug makers in *Teotitlan de Valle* spoke Zapotec, not Spanish. We watched them brush wool and spin it into yarn, turning the wheel with one hand while holding the ball of raw wool in the other. Red strands were draped over a fence to dry. The color came from ground-up dead worms found in nopales leaves. Yellow was made by boiling dried moss, blue from cactus, black from a woody bean-like plant. The rug makers crafted sixteen colors to weave into their rugs. We were entranced. Rick saw opportunity as an importer with sales outlets in the U.S. but I didn't want to work, I wanted to look, touch and savor and not return to the United States.

We had dinner on the second-floor balcony of a restaurant overlooking *Oaxaca*'s central square. Leafy trees spread a canopy over the ambling crowds below. They were young and old, Mexicans and Europeans. A band played. Bow-tied *Mariachis* strolled among the tables and Rick bought me a gardenia.

We reluctantly boarded a train to Mexico City and took a bus back to the boat, planning the next trip.

Golf got us off the boat, too. We put our travel-size bags in the dinghy, splashed ashore, dried our feet and with gear slung over our shoulders walked to the main road. It wasn't necessary to speak the language, every bus driver knew we wanted a golf course and told us where our stop was. We took the bus to golf courses up and down the west coast of Mexico.

In Ixtapa, my caddy, Martin, told me he wanted to take his family on vacation to the United States but couldn't get a travel visa. Evidently, the United States was afraid he might stay. I thought about that. I was allowed to visit his country but he couldn't get the paperwork to take his kids to Disneyland and the Grand Canyon.

I was left with an image of American lawmakers vacationing in Mexico for a few weeks in an attempt to replicate the life that Martin has. He lives in paradise. He has a job that he loves. Yet, Americans fear he'll be intrigued by our clogged freeways, low-paying jobs and long hours.

With Martin's help, I played well that day.

Anchored in the bay at *Las Hadas*, we lounged at the hotel swimming pool and overheard a conversation. Two seats were available in a van headed to a golf course the next morning. So at 7:00 on New Year's Day we met in the lobby to play at *El Tamarindo*. It was like playing golf in a zoo with more toucans and monkeys than putts. A too long approach sent the ball over the cliff into the Pacific Ocean. I ran out of golf balls.

And fate was taking me back out to sea.

> *"In the middle of difficulty lies opportunity."*
> ALBERT EINSTEIN

CHAPTER 19
The Storm

A FIST OF wind knocked us hard to starboard.

Rick yelled, "Release, Release!" while he leapt onto the cabin roof to reef the main. I wasn't a novice anymore and my fingers were already wrapped around the white braided line. I yanked it out of the jaws of the cleat and it sang as the tension eased and the huge sail flapped like a giant's laundry. With the sail rendered powerless, *Nanook* snapped upright.

I attached my safety harness, braced the tiller with my leg and steered into the wind. I yanked on my gloves and wrapped the jib line around the winch and began cranking. With the forward sail de-powered, too, when the next gust hit we stayed upright. I took four long, hard pulls on the roller furling lines before the jib was wound neatly around the forestay.

With only a reduced mainsail up, we lunged through

the growing waves. My eyes sought Rick's. And stayed. With his free hand he brushed salt spray from his short brown hair and new beard. The familiar gesture was comforting.

With the sails set to handle the rough seas and the self-steering keeping us on a jerky course, we went below and stripped out of our soaked T-shirts and shorts. I wrung them out in the sink and hung them in the head. Dressed in dry shorts and T-shirt Rick sat at the nav station checking the charts. I towel-dried my short hair and put on a long T-shirt and shorts before clamping two pots to the gimbaled stove. I splashed some olive oil in one, filled the other with water and turned on the propane.

Rick tuned the SSB radio to the weather report. My knife against the chopping block matched the tempo of the recorded weather report. Static interfered but not so badly that we didn't hear the dismal outlook. Rick adjusted the dials but it didn't help. My hands were busy but my mind prayed that we were in an isolated squall, not the beginning of something bigger.

I dumped damp onions in the pan and olive oil spat back at me. Rick patted my fanny on his way back to the cockpit. "That smells great, honey, thanks for doing it." The smell of garlic and onions blended with the salt air and steam rose from the pan of water waiting for the spiral noodles.

Rick tended the sails and watched the horizon. When I handed Rick his bowl of noodles, with vegetables and leftover dorado tossed in, he stood under the cover of the dodger with his legs braced but arms relaxed to keep the contents from spilling on his bare feet. The warm bowl and its steamy contents were aromatherapy at sea.

Too soon the wind picked up speed like a train leaving the city. The waves curdled and clouds stretched into streamers that turned to charcoal. Warm rain splattered the deck like shards of glass. He didn't need to say it, I could tell by his face, body language and the sea conditions. But he said it anyway. "Honey, this looks bad."

While Rick cranked down the starboard portholes, I checked the port side, sealing each opening against rain and waves. We tossed our clean shirts on the bed to keep them dry and wearing only shorts, buckled ourselves into our safety harnesses and scrambled back into the cockpit.

Nanook twisted and pitched in the chaotic seas. The lines squawked like angry crows and Rick hollered above the bellowing wind, "Bring the storm sail forward!" My hair was already plastered to my face from the pelting rain. I dragged the bulky bag behind me, crawling on my hands and knees through the narrow alley toward the bow. Together, we wrestled the stiff sail out of the bag and hanked it onto the stay. *Nanook* struggled like a dolphin tangled in a net.

On shore, television announcers might have described the danger and given the hurricane a name, but on the ocean, we didn't have television and her name was irrelevant.

Nanook shouldered into the steep waves that tossed

us like a bathtub toy. We took turns on storm watch, two hours on duty and two hours off. I was wrapped in exhaustion when day two arrived with a barely perceptible distinction between the dark gray of night and the lighter gray of daytime. Everything was the hue of tarnished silver.

On the third day, blue and white cracks appeared in a spackled sky. The birds released their grip from our spreaders and circled tentatively. While soup bubbled on the stove I opened the locker where I stored the ceramic pitcher Rick had given me for our anniversary. I gently unwrapped the white towel that protected it. I traced its smooth edges with my fingers. Relieved that it had survived the violent thrashing, I nestled it back in its storage space.

When the downpour thinned to a steady drizzle, the roaring wind quieted. Clouds lay in shreds and the towering seas gave way to long rollers. I handed Rick a mug of steaming soup.

The sun peeked out and dried the decks. We hung wet clothes on the lifelines, where they flapped like flags of surrender. Rick held me in his arms and I sobbed out my pent-up nerves. Torn clouds stretched like gauze over a wound and the VHF radio announced that the hurricane did have a name. It was Rick.

In the four years we'd been in Mexico, Rick and I had been through a half dozen nights on anchor watch when the weather had changed as well as a dozen other terrors. Whether it was the seas kicking up unexpectedly, an important piece of *Nanook*'s equipment breaking or falling overboard, or the wind, we had remained upbeat about our chosen time-out. Until now.

The sky looked like a bruise. Shades of purple stretched to dark black, interrupted by circles of pale yellow. To an English teacher, the storm is the point in the story where everything changes. King Lear went insane. E.T. phoned home. Rick and I opened the forbidden subject. Should we sell *Nanook* and find a different way to see the world?

We talked about the changes that living on a sailboat had brought to our lives, about our love for each other and the special times spent exploring Mexican villages. And we admitted out loud how little we knew about sailing.

That week something happened to me besides surviving the storm. A realization crept in as stealthily as sea water seeped through the sealed port holes. I accepted that we weren't going to sail to the Marquesas, to Australia and to Turkey. Or even through the Panama Canal.

Rick was embattled by too many hours in the engine room. Our creeping pace drove him crazy. Lots of our cruising pals had gone home, replaced by a freshman class of dreamers. We were no longer freshmen but we couldn't go home because we didn't have one. We didn't have the kind of budget that could afford both a home and a boat. I was raw and questioning, confused about how to continue to travel and explore if we sold *Nanook*. The idea of returning to a normal life was like a heat rash.

When we had first rounded *Cabo San Lucas* on our

approach to mainland Mexico, we met a couple who had been underway for just two weeks. They announced a yard sale of sorts on the Net. Everything that wasn't bolted down or mandatory to run the boat had been for sale and so was their boat. I didn't want to get strength from quitting on our dream because someone else quit after just a handful of days, but it was a slight satisfaction.

We hadn't mastered the itinerary we'd set for ourselves but we'd had an intriguing journey. Now I wondered what lay ahead.

In the morning, four dolphins arrived, turning in a great circle around us. These beasts of good omen played with our bow wake. Their shiny gray backs crossed back and forth at our bow, diving in and out as if they were braiding a rope with their snouts. They twirled and tangoed, dove and played, seeming to tow us for most of the day.

A SINGLE STAR shone when I wrote by the light of a flashlight propped on a cushion. The ink on paper, caught in the beam, illuminated the words with the glow of neon.

> This voyage I'm on is one of discovery, the discovery of me. Choosing life on this little sailboat was a choice in favor of experiencing life first hand. It

has taught me that there are no guarantees. There's just life, to be lived as fully as possible.

There are times when we feel an instinct to reach out and move to the frontiers for new experiences. Our ancestors sailed across the ocean for a fresh start in a new country. Others crossed the plains in covered wagons. Astronauts feel the need to explore the solar system.

Throughout a lifetime, there are moments of decision. Choosing a college, buying a home, having a child. Whether to stay home and tend to the known or to take a risk and jump into the unknown. One choice doesn't have more validity than the other. At this time in my life choosing the safe way wouldn't have been constructive. I needed to test myself in order to grow.

Thoreau must have known this when he moved to Walden Pond and wrote, "I went to the woods because I wished to live deliberately, to front only the essential facts in life and see if I could not learn what it had to teach and not, when I came to die, discover that I had not lived."

Sailing away was the equivalent of Walden for me.

> *"They always say time changes things, but you actually have to change them yourself."*
>
> ANDY WARHOL

CHAPTER 20
Changing Course

WHILE WE WERE away my parents bought a new house and moved. Rick's mother died. AJ and Lisa graduated from college and my father had a stroke. Life went on and so did death. We went back to the United States for some of the occasions, missed some and put more coins in pay phones during those times. But we didn't change our plans.

Now, perched on top of a mirror, the sails flapped in the absence of wind. Despite hiring mechanics, dismantling the engine and replacing parts, our engine still overheated. It was a lousy partner. Our circumnavigation had taken on the characteristics of Saint Rita, the patron saint of impossible dreams.

I wrote:

> The sea is an unpredictable lover. One brief moment of inattention, one miscalculation or

> equipment failure is the difference between life and death. I prefer periods of calm, when terror is parked on a distant lot. I think I'm ready to live where I can write, make friends who stay put and do more sports, too.

I had learned to sail but the cruising life was far from an ideal fit for our strengths and weaknesses. I got scared when the wind blew too hard. Rick dropped parts overboard and was clumsy cleaning fish and working in small spaces. I'd gotten used to wet clothes and no refrigerator but the leaky portholes annoyed me and the diesel pissed me off. And storms were a bigger level of discomfort.

If a sailboat rolled over I knew that she'd right herself; my brain knew that *Nanook* was designed that way, that our heavy keel would pop us upright. Always. Despite the knowledge, an image of Rick's bleeding body floating away had painted itself on my consciousness and wouldn't erase. That particular terror was stamped on my soul.

Alternately arguing, hugging and shedding tears, we agreed to sell *Nanook*. Like a balloon string slipping out of a child's grasp, there was nothing I could do but watch the dream vanish.

We'd gone sailing because the man I loved needed a change and I wanted to change. It's a minor difference when you write it but to an English teacher the distinction is huge. Rick wanted to do something different. I wanted to be someone different. We had accomplished both.

I had trusted Rick to take good care of me and agreed to be his enthusiastic partner in the new life he sought. We trusted each other enough to go and loved each other enough to quit.

"Looks like we'll see the Panama Canal and Turkey from a cruise ship or as crew on someone else's boat, Honey," Rick said.

"I think you're right. But it makes me a little sad." I replied.

Rick hugged me. "Don't be. It'll be an adventure," he said with a wink.

"Does that mean we should open the Equator crossing wine now?"

"No time like the present. You steer, I'll get it."

We kissed while we traded places and Rick went below. After a few minutes, I wasn't the least bit surprised when his muffled voice drifted into the cockpit. "Where is it?"

I smiled at the back of his red faded swim trunks bent over double, his head deep in the locker on the starboard side. Some things don't change. "Port side, behind the center cushion, not underneath," I called.

Rick turned and opened the locker. "Ah hah," he said, pulling out a 1981 *Domaine de Chevalier* wrapped in a blue kitchen towel. "Not too much worse for the wear," he said, examining the bottle.

He returned to the cockpit with the towel over his arm, two plastic wine glasses and the bottle we'd been saving since our wedding day. The label was faded and torn. The cork crumbled at his touch.

"This cork held up about as well as our itinerary," he said.

"But like us, it can be salvaged." I went below and found a strainer.

Rick poured red wine through the sieve and handed me a glass while he sniffed his.

"A touch of vinegar, blue cheese and old socks, a vintage year," he said in a credible impression of a stuffy sommelier.

I put my nose to the rim of my glass. "Well, it's a toast to endings. May we have many."

"What does that mean?"

"It means that you have to start before you can stop. If we spend the next twenty years toasting endings that means we'll start lots of good adventures, too." I took a cautious sip. "It's not that bad."

"Neither are you," Rick said. We put our glasses down, wrapped our arms around each other and surveyed our surroundings. "I don't want to sound too corny, but to quote Jimmy Buffett, "It's been a lovely cruise."

Aborting our circumnavigation without crossing an ocean didn't feel like failure. Like the movie line from *Jerry Maguire*, when he expressed his love in a long-winded speech to Dorothy, her reply was the simple phrase: "You had me at hello." The idea of going cruising had grabbed me when the idea was born. I wasn't the least bit sorry we'd taken the plunge.

Two days later, we were anchored in fifteen feet of

gently rippling turquoise. The sound of Yanni filled the air. I held a tumbler of *Ron Oscuro*, warm dark rum, in my left hand, a pen in my right and a journal on my lap. I rewound our sailing years like a DVD spinning scenes, searching for a defining moment.

Gasping noises from the water startled me and I jumped up, knocking the journal to the deck. Hundreds of dolphins had crept up to surprise me. I put down the rum and pen, wiping tears from my cheeks. Had they come to perform a final act before we pulled the curtain on our cruising life?

"Will I ever be this happy again?" I wondered.

Giving the thought some perspective, I rationalized, "If nothing else measures up, at least I've been here."

Part of the magic in going sailing was the commitment that quitting our jobs and selling the house signified. It defied society's expectations. Somewhere deep inside me a rebel from the 1960s had been hiding. She'd apparently just been too busy being good to act out until now.

I'd swum with dolphins and danced with blue-footed boobies. We'd walked in a Christmas candlelight procession on cobbled streets and learned to speak some Spanish. Returning to the suburbs was going to be an empty substitute and I cringed at the thought.

I would miss the music of my life at sea: Being awakened by birds on shore, cawing and honking a noisy "Good morning." Lying in my bunk, listening to dolphins rattle the anchor chain. The American flag rustling on the stern.

We spent the day reading and being lazy before we

swam to shore. We talked about what shape our lives might take without *Nanook*. Rick switches gears easily but I could hear mine grinding. Walking across the salt flats, I pocketed more seashells than usual.

We discussed ideas of affordable adventures. Dusting off old ideas and conjuring up new ones, we reshuffled the deck. I had said at the outset that the next decade was Rick's and a few of those years still yawned in front of us.

We had met a cruising couple on *Scout* who told us their story about sailing Mexican waters in the winter and motorcycling through Europe each summer. We batted their idea around until intrigue turned to infection. We would buy a motorcycle, ship it to Europe and camp, exploring for one long summer.

WHEN *NANOOK* HAD new owners there was an audible

sigh. She had been our only home for six years, four of those in Mexico.

Legend says that the happiest two days in a boater's life are the day you buy it and the day it's sold. The sigh from my parents sounded more like relief. At last, they presumed, we would return to our responsibilities, buy a house, get jobs and be normal. Rick and I were happy because we were ready to begin the next adventure.

My family had taken vacations. to Hawaii, Palm Springs, the Oregon coast and Yellowstone National Park. My father liked to say, "We took the kids camping once; we stayed in the Lodge." I was about to take off on another adventure for which I had no background of experience.

Our daughters were enthusiastic. Even though our ideas still came as a surprise to me, AJ and Lisa expected us to wander and thought it was pretty cool that their parents were shopping for a tent and a motorcycle. They had grown from students to adults in our absence.

AJ worked in a television news room on the East Coast and Lisa taught Special Ed on the West Coast. Rick and I were proud of their focus and relieved that they had health insurance, even though we still did not.

Without Nanook, we also didn't have a home base, so we bought an early 1990s Airstream trailer because her vintage shape appealed to us. The salesman commented on the small size of the refrigerator but it looked cavernous to me. Our first night in a campground we joked that the anchor wouldn't drag in our new life on wheels but I don't think we were really joking.

The moon was different that night. It shone like a spotlight, giving a silver edge to the clouds. In the back of our new long-bed pickup truck that towed the Airstream sat a proud and shiny red motorcycle, a BMW R1100GS. It would need bigger saddle bags and a taller windshield. We needed camping gear and Europe travel guides. Again, we had lots to learn.

> "The universe is one great kindergarten for man.... The mountain teaches stability and grandeur; the ocean immensity and change."
>
> ORISON SWETT MARDEN

EPILOGUE
Patterns from Scraps

I CHANGED IN small increments as our time at sea grew. Like a jeweler tapping his forging hammer, the events of our time-out shaped a new me. If suburbia had enshrouded me in pervasive fog, confining me to its expectations, going sailing burned off the fog and opened my eyes to new possibilities.

With each nautical mile something in me loosened, the way a knot loosens. It unleashed a woman who could rise out of her fears. I learned that tears are healing. What soap was for my body, tears did for my soul.

And I discovered that I could travel without big suitcases. I'm the only one who cares what I'm wearing and I didn't need a pile of skirts, scarves and shoes to weigh me down.

We made our own rules and relished in the freedom.

We ate when we were hungry. We wore what we wanted or nothing at all.

I grew accustomed to color: orange fleshy melons, fuchsia papayas and pungent limes. Swags of red, green and yellow chili peppers. Houses splashed in primary colors marching up hillsides, flanked by hedges of brilliant bougainvillea. At daybreak, color threaded the sky and stitched it together again at sunset. Every day was a walk through God's gallery and I vowed never to return to the blandness of beige walls.

The child who had longed to color outside the lines began to scribble with abandon. Having discovered that child, I vowed to hold her hand, keeping her close..

The idea of "home" changed from an address to a place to put my head for the night. I became a turtle, carrying my home with me as I wandered.

When AmyJean and Christopher announced their engagement, the question was where to have the wedding? They decided that it would be wherever *Nanook* was moored and we all thought that would be in the Caribbean. Instead we pulled off a destination wedding in *Zihuatanejo*. Rick got a mail-order minister's license. We took over an inn on a cliff overlooking the bay and hired a mariachi band. Family, friends, and the bride and groom partied for a full week. On one dinghy ride to shore, with the wedding party waiting on the beach, we caught the dinghy sideways in the surf and rolled. Rick lost his glasses; we were soaked and sandy but the wedding went on.

Life in Mexico taught me that efficiency shouldn't trump delight. I bought fresh food from local vendors and lost my American supermarket habit of buying unripe fruit. Shopping in a foreign language for foods I didn't know how to cook made me conscious of new ways to train an old model.

The horizon stretched to infinity and that, too, changed my view. *Nanook* was an insignificant swatch of fiberglass on an immense canvas. The ocean taught me I could control neither time nor destiny. There were rough seas and periods of calm. The key to a good life was the ability to float between the two, learning from the troughs as well as the crests and enjoying the ride. If I'd had a sense of self importance before the trip, sailing shut it down.

Sailing gave me time to think, to write and to process my feelings. The decades before we left had whipped by in a busy blur. The ocean forced me to slow down. I learned to appreciate the civility of a siesta; I didn't need a frantic pace to be worthwhile. I pledged to maintain a quiet calendar with lots of white space when I returned to a land life.

The culture of my childhood was the opposite of the life I lived in Mexico. I'd been raised to think of leisurely lunches and life in the slow lane as recipes for failure. Even rambling conversations were outlawed in my youth. We were supposed to use language, as well as time, efficiently. Life on a slow boat taught me that these are not inviolable laws. There is no moral high road that dictates how a life should be lived. A quality life can be lived *muy lentamente*.

Another belief that was part of my upbringing held that the only way to be successful was to look forward. "Don't talk about the past," Dad said while Mom prattled on about someone, somewhere, who did something yesterday, or last month. The future was the only topic worthy of discussion. My life wasn't like that. Rick and I had long rambling talks while the boat moved slowly across the ocean. We discussed magnificent as well as minor moments. No subject was off limits. We turned events over, holding them in our hands, examining them like underwater treasures. With only each other for company, our relationship moved from wonderful to miraculous.

And I found out that I didn't miss my chance at the ideal career. My destiny was to be a mother. A really good one. In that job, the logistics of everyone else had set my schedule. I'd been a passenger in my life but now I sit firmly in the driver's seat. I'm a grandmother and a writer as well as a mom to married daughters with lives of their own.

I realized, too, that it was because of, not in spite of, a childhood in the Land of Oz that I could abandon my home, job and predictable patterns. My parents had so adequately nurtured my self-image that I had the confidence to leave because I didn't fear starting over.

Cruising led me to gems that aren't stocked in jewelry stores. I found seashells so delicate that when I got back to *Nanook*, I wrapped them in tissue for safekeeping. I wondered how such fragile shapes could arrive at my feet in perfect condition after traveling across oceans on the backs of the waves. On one walk, I collected sand dollars so huge we called it "frisbee beach." And I found a turtle shell, abandoned by its owner as if he'd just walked out and scuttled on. They were all gifts from the sea.

Cruisers had the luxury of time and we invested it wisely. Sailing in warm waters was an incubator for personalities with a common purpose and like short love affairs, our friendships were passionate and high-octane encounters. I learned the value of meeting interesting people and making friends, regardless of how soon we might part company.

Going sailing unraveled my tightly knit expectations, revealing the colorful threads of a new tapestry. Being away from everything we had known forced us to rely on each other. That much alone time might be dangerous for a normal couple, but we were lucky, with a solid understanding of each other's strengths and limits. We were blessed to have a magical love that grew stronger as our time at sea lengthened. Rick was and is both my mainsail and my anchor.

Packing our belongings off *Nanook*, a ragged piece of paper fell out of a journal. It smelled of the sea and the ink was wrinkled by water stains.

> Life on a small sailboat in a big ocean stripped me of my bubble wrap, exposing raw skin to salt air.

Now, I pedaled my folding bicycle behind Rick. On the back of his red baseball hat, stitched in bold blue letters, it said "Ride slow." I watched the writing rise and fall as he pumped the pedals up the hill. The bobbing letters were right. "Slow" is a good way to live.

LaVergne, TN USA
16 September 2010
197302LV00002B/2/P